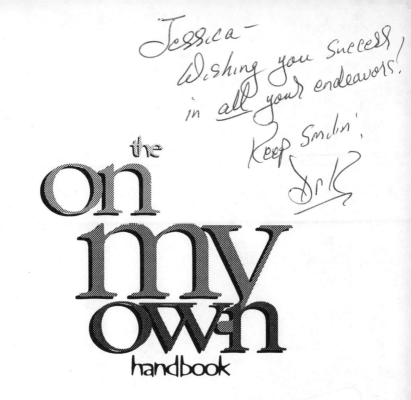

the
on
my
own
handbook

bobb biehl

Chariot VICTOR
PUBLISHING
A DIVISION OF COOK COMMUNICATIONS

The On My Own Handbook

Victor Books is an imprint of ChariotVictor Publishing,
a division of Cook Communications, Colorado Springs, Colorado, 80918
Cook Communications, Paris, Ontario
Kingsway Communications, Eastbourne, England

THE ON MY OWN HANDBOOK
© 1991 by Bobb Biehl

Cover design by Bill Coburn
Interior illustrations by Scot McDonald
Cover photo by Stuart Westmorland - Stock Imagery

Second Edition, 1997
Printed in Canada
00 99 98 97   10

Library of Congress Cataloging in Publication Data

Biehl, Bobb
    The On My Own Handbook/ by Bobb Biehl
    p.   cm.
    ISBN 1-55513-335-5
    1. Young adults—United States—Life skills guides.   2. Young
adults—United States—Religious life. I. Title
HQ799.B54 1991
305.23'5—dc20   91-25342
                                                     CIP

I would like to express my sincere thanks to my son, J. Ira Biehl, for the inspiration for this book and for his invaluable input in the financial section.

Thank you, J.

TABLE OF CONTENTS

INTRODUCTION

INTRODUCTION

Have you ever asked yourself, "Am I learning everything I need to know to be a wise, balanced, successful adult?" Your parents, teachers, church leaders, and other concerned adults have no doubt been trying to prepare you to face the world. But until you get involved with preparing *yourself*, you'll never be confident to move ahead with life on your own.

The On My Own Handbook has been written to help you answer the previous question with a confident "Yes!" It is a collection of short principles that include stories, questions, and personal application to help you remember lifelong truths. And since everyone learns a little differently, you will be able to adapt everything to your own personal style.

I hope you won't see this book as just "one more thing I have to do." The idea of learning principles may sound a bit like doing homework, but everything here has been written with the sole purpose of helping you have a more successful life. This book can be a helpful tool to give you confidence as you grow into adulthood. You might even want to make learning these principles a family project. Your parents will have much to offer as you gather information that will help you all for the rest of your lives.

And even if you have already left home, it's not too late to learn anything from *The On My Own Handbook*. You'll find good, new information, as well as some worthwhile reminders that you'll want to absorb and maybe even pass along to future generations.

11

HOW TO MAKE THE MOST OF THIS BOOK

The key to success in using this book is to apply each principle to your own life situation. One book cannot address every specific circumstance. You may be 15; you may be 25. You may be headed for college, or trade school, or the job market. You may or may not be close to your family. So it's up to you make appropriate applications for each principle in this book.

First, read the principle and the explanation. Then spend a few moments figuring how it applies to you personally. Learn to think creatively. Recall illustrations from your family life, from business or work situations, from school, from your relationships, and so forth. Then move on to the Key Questions and Action Point, completing each phase. When you think you fully understand the principle, move on to the next one.

You need not take these principles in order. Feel free to skip from section to section to find help for whatever is on your mind on any particular day. There is a checklist of principles in the back of the book, so when you complete a principle, be sure to check it off and keep up with your progress.

I once heard a popular seminar teacher say, "Anything you read 90 times, you've memorized whether you wanted to or not." I agree. Think back to records you liked a lot when you were younger. You can probably still sing along, even though you may not have listened to them for years. That's because you probably heard the songs 90 times or more. Whether or not you planned to memorize a particular song, it's still in your memory. (I find myself singing along with the "Smokin' Oldies" on a local radio station that only plays the first ten years of rock 'n' roll!)

Thirty years from now you will find yourself quoting many of the principles you put into your memory today. The wisdom you gather will return to give helpful perspective when you're clear across the country, or on the other side of the world.

Some things you learn now will stick; others won't. But as you learn these principles, pray and leave it up to God to bring them back to memory at a time when you need them during your adult years.

One of the main benefits of this kind of book is that you can go at your own pace. If you simply keep chipping away at the principles, you'll be done before you realize it. ("One by one, soon you're done!") Don't feel pressure to whip through this book as soon as you can. It's much better to take your time and feel a sense of completion, progress, and accomplishment.

WHY WRITE *THE ON MY OWN HANDBOOK?*

As you read through this book, you may wonder what prompted me to write it. The idea was actually born when my son J. (his full name is J. Ira Biehl, named after his great-great grandfather) was in the sixth grade. It seemed like every time I turned around, J. needed a dollar or two for legitimate needs—skateboard parts, movies, bike tires, clothes, going out with friends, etc. I didn't want to just hand him money, because I felt he would appreciate it more if he had to work for it. Yet when I tried to help him find ways to make money, it didn't turn out to be as easy as when I was growing up.

When I was 12 or 13, I lived in Mancelona, Michigan, a small rural village where I could always get a paper route, hoe corn for my grandfather, or pick cherries for my uncle to make a few dollars. Most kids growing up in an urban area today don't have the same opportunities to earn money.

Where I live today, we have a fairly small lot. We have no lawn to keep up, so J. couldn't even mow the grass to make extra money. Then one day I came up with an idea. I could teach him the principles I teach Christian leaders in my consulting practice around the country. I was willing to shell out a few dollars to motivate him to learn principles that would help him for a lifetime.

One day when he got home from school, I asked, "J., how would you like to earn $300 or more?"

He gave me a look as if to ask, "Who would I have to kill?"

I continued, "What I'd like you to do is learn some principles."

Of course, in the sixth grade you're not even sure what the word "principle" means. So I explained, "These are just sayings—wise things people have taught me or that I've learned over the years. They're short, but if you learn them they will help you under-stand

13

a lot about why things work the way they do."

J.'s excitement grew. "Sure, I'll learn them. How much money do I get?"

Responding to his enthusiasm to better himself, I explained the plan: "I'll give you a dollar a principle the first time you learn these hundred principles. That's a hundred dollars. The second time through, I'll give you 75 cents each. The third time, 50 cents. The fourth time, 25 cents. And the fifth time, if you can say them all perfectly, top to bottom, I'll give you a $100 bonus."

At this point, I added a few conditions. "You need to memorize at least five principles at a time. That's so you don't just come in and say, 'Here's a principle; I need a dollar.' You need to sit down and spend time to understand each of them, because I will expect you to: (1) Recite each principle, word for word; (2) Tell me what it means in your own words; and (3) Give me an example of how you could use the principle in your everyday life."

The first time through, J. took about six months to get through the principles. The second time through took an additional five or six months. The third time took three or four months. As a result, every time we went through the principles, his illustrations changed. He was learning each principle at a deeper and deeper level. By the time we finished, he'd gone through each of the hundred principles five times, applying them in very, very different ways each time. As an adult, the principles are now deeply embedded into his memory.

When I told this story to David Orris and Paul Mouw at David C. Cook, they asked if I could help them pass this idea and the many principles on to young people like you. *The On My Own Handbook* is the result.

MOTIVATION FOR LEARNING PRINCIPLES

With J., using money was a real motivation to get him to learn and apply these principles. Maybe you can work out a similar deal with your parents. If not, don't give up. Just knowing that these truths will guide you through the hard times in your life should be motivation enough. Then it becomes more a challenge of finding the right time and place to learn them.

For example, think of how often you complain of being bored. If, instead of making life miserable for the people around you, you learned a principle instead, your boring times will be kept to a minimum.

Or think of those family vacation travel days that get so long and restless! As your family is traveling, learning principles can be a good way to take advantage of "dead" time.

Every person has a different motivational "on button." Think about how you are motivated, and use the system that works for you.

I anticipate that *The On My Own Handbook* will not be just a learning experience for you, but for your entire family as well. I hope your family will have an experience similar to that of my wife Cheryl and I. Prior to J.'s 18th birthday, I wrote to about 120 friends and asked them to send him a one-page letter that included three principles they wanted to teach their own children.

We got back 70 or so letters, put them in a leather binder, and gave it to J. for his birthday. One thing I did not expect was how much Cheryl and I learned by reading the letters from those wise people who shared the best of their thinking. Hopefully these principles will be a learning experience for you as well as your parents and family members.

FAMILY HEIRLOOM

As you're working through this book, feel free to add principles of your own—things your parents (and others) have taught you that you feel are important. Ask your parents the most important things they wanted to teach you while you were growing up and what principles they would like to see you teach their grandchildren.

By adding your own principles, you create a family heirloom that can be passed along to future generations. Not only will your children benefit from your wisdom, but your grandchildren and your great-grandchildren as well.

Principles are mini-statements of cause and effect. Collect principles because they help explain why things do or do not work.

Throughout our lifetimes we come across simple sentences or quotes which explain why or how something works. Such statements help us understand things more clearly. Unfortunately, very few people collect these sayings, quotes, observations, rules of thumb, and principles.

Principles are mini-statements of cause and effect. Cause and effect means simply this: something causes things to happen, from which there is an effect. For example, wind causes the trees to shake, and heat causes water to boil.

For a quote to truly qualify as a principle, it must be a mini-statement of cause and effect. "If you do this, then that happens." By this definition, not all of the 100 statements contained in this book are technically principles. This book is intended more to be a collection of wisdom. So included with the "official" principles will be rules of thumb, old sayings, and various bits of truth on a variety of subjects—all of which I hope will be helpful to you.

COLLECT PRINCIPLES

When I was about 25, it occurred to me that I was hearing a lot of wise things from my parents, grandparents, uncles, aunts, cousins, teachers, etc. Why not have a notebook or someplace to write them down so I would never forget them? Then when I needed to make a decision about something, it would be like all of my friends and family members were with me, trying to help me solve the problem!

Begin collecting principles. Over your lifetime they will help you solve problems, understand life, and make you a better person.

WHY THINGS DO AND DON'T WORK

Here's an example of a principle from Dr. Peter F. Drucker: "Once the facts are clear, the decisions jump out at you." (This is principle #54 in this book.)

Doesn't it make sense that if a decision isn't obvious to you in a given situation, it's simply because the facts aren't clear? The "clear facts" are the *cause*. The *effect* is that "the decisions jump out at you."

For example, let's say you and your friends are trying to decide whether or not to go to a ball game. One fact that would help you make the decision is whether or not you have enough money to go. If as a group you have $30, and $10 will get you all in, then going is an option. But if it takes $30 to go to the game and you only have $10 between you, your decision becomes pretty clear!

A list of principles will be valuable when you're an adult. Principles provide not only creative alternatives for decisions, but also objectivity. I've found that my collection of principles helps me consider many perspectives in a very short amount of time.

WHERE DO I START?

When it occurred to me that collecting principles would be a smart thing to do, I grabbed paper and a pencil and started to write all the principles I already knew. I tried to remember what I had learned from relatives, friends, books, professors, etc. In a few hours I came up with 162 principles! Ever since then I've been collecting and gathering additional principles to have available whenever I'm stuck on a problem.

I encourage you to do the same. Begin with the principles in this book, add the ones you have gathered on your own, and keep collecting. You'll be glad you did. Sometimes in the middle of the night when I can't sleep because my mind is on some idea or problem, I get out my list and go through it. I often get many ideas as I apply different principles to the same problem. New solutions, new ideas, and new alternatives come out that I didn't even imagine before.

I sometimes imagine I'm at a huge oval conference table with my friends, professors, and relatives (represented by my collection of principles). I imagine saying to them, "Today the problem is how to write a book." Then I go around and "discuss" the situation with each "person."

The first person says, "How could you write a better book by *asking*?" The second says, "Have you made the correct *assumptions*?" The third asks, "What does the *Bible* say about it?" The fourth says, "What's the *context or comparison* for the book?" The next says, "What are the *facts* you need for the book?" And on it goes.

Do you see how it works? Anything you try to do—from writing a book to running for class president to finding the right job—you can do better by reviewing all the principles you've been taught. They will reveal possibilities you may not have considered.

Obviously not every principle applies every time, but all you need to do is *consider* each one. If it doesn't apply, move on. If it does, then it may bring a totally different perspective than you would get otherwise.

KEY QUESTIONS

1. *What are some principles you know right now?*
2. *Where is the best place for you to collect principles—in a notebook, workbook, a box, a filing cabinet, etc.?*
3. *Where could you get other principles, sayings, or rules of thumb?*

ACTION POINT

Get a paper and a pencil and write down all the principles you know. Try to remember what you have been taught by relatives, friends, family, books you've read, tapes you've listened to, seminars you've attended, classes you've had, and so forth. Think hard, because these principles will work for you for a long time to come!

Everything in life fits into one of seven basic categories: Family/Marriage, Financial, Personal Growth, Physical, Professional/Career, Social, or Spiritual.

PRINCIPLE

2

I've heard from a number of adults as well as teenagers who are trying to makes sense of their lives, who feel overwhelmed at the scope of everything they are facing. The complexity of life can certainly cause confusion and uncertainty!

About fifteen years ago I began trying to figure out how life could be sorted into categories. As I began studying and experimenting, I found that nearly everything we experience in life fits into one of the seven areas.

(1) *Family/Marriage*—This category includes the issues that have to do with either the family you grew up in, or your own family (spouse and children).

(2) *Financial*—This is a major category because it involves everything to do with money. It includes many dimensions, such as risks, investments, loans, and so forth.

(3) *Personal Growth*—This area refers to how you grow as an individual. It will include all the self-help books you read, the seminars you attend, the counseling you get, the trips you take, and similar specific events.

(4) *Physical*—This includes all the exercising you do, medical checkups you get, hospitalizations, sports activities, etc.

(5) *Professional/Career*—This category includes your education, all your jobs, and so forth.

(6) *Social*—This area includes parties, relationships, and how you keep in touch with all your friends.

(7) *Spiritual Dimensions*—This important category pertains to your involvements with church, Bible study, devotional life, Christian service, and so forth.

HOW TO USE THESE CATEGORIES

Some events can fit into more than one category, in which case you should decide which area is of primary importance to you. You may wonder what difference it makes whether or not all the things you experience fit into seven categories. Consider this: Let's say you're thinking about whether to go to college. You're trying to decide between going to a university or staying home and working. Without some method of evaluating the benefits of going to college, you could think about the implications of your decision in many ways.

A couple of your friends with no plans for the future might convince you to stay at home and bum around with them. Or if you love your car but would have to leave it at home, you might make your decision based on this limited information.

On the other hand, you could consider the implications of this decision in the seven basic areas of life: What difference will going to college make to my family? What will be the financial costs? How will I grow personally? What are the physical implications? The career implications? The social implications? The spiritual implications? By just considering the decision in light of all seven categories, you will consider many implications within a short time.

It's also important to see that each of the areas ultimately affects the other six. Every priority you place in the physical category may weaken the other areas. If you spend an hour jogging, you can't spend it with your family. If you spend it making money, you may not be able to stay in shape physically. Every area affects every other area!

LIFE IS A STRUGGLE FOR BALANCE

As you try to grow in seven different categories, it is easy to get out of balance. But how do you do a balance check? How do you make sure you don't neglect one area and overdo another?

One way to maintain balance in life is to regularly rate each of the seven areas by asking yourself, "On a scale of 1 to 10, how happy am I with each of these areas?" For example, how would you rate yourself as a family member? How would you rate yourself financially at this time? How is your physical development coming along? And so forth. Let's say you rate 9 or 10 in all of the categories except one. If in that one area you rate about a 2, you probably need work in that category. The seven dimensions are a quick way to keep a check on your balance in life.

The seven areas also form a clear framework for balanced goal setting. One way to make sure you're setting balanced goals is to set one goal in each of the categories to accomplish during the next 90 days. You only need to set seven goals to feel like you've got life pretty well covered.

The principles that follow in this book are categorized into the seven areas of life, though in no particular order. If you feel the need to begin in one of the areas, then do so. Focus on the category where you need help. Or if you want to, examine one principle from each area and keep bouncing around. But I encourage you to develop some sort of systematic way to go through this book. As you apply these principles to your specific situations and problems, you will find solutions and gain the confidence you will need as you prepare to live on your own. And that will be well worth your effort.

KEY QUESTIONS
1. *Do you feel balanced at this point in life? If not, where is the imbalance?*
2. *What major decision do you need to make during the next month? How should you look at this decision in light of the seven areas of life?*
3. *On a scale of 1 to 10, how would you rate your life in each of the seven areas? In which area do you need the most work?*

ACTION POINT
Set one realistic, measurable goal to accomplish in each of the seven areas during the next 90 days. (Don't be too ambitious at first.) Mark your calendar and be sure to follow up on how you did.

FAMILY/MARRIAGE

PRINCIPLES

There is a huge difference between true love and "puppy love." Puppy love says, "You meet my needs." True love asks, "How can I meet your needs?"

PRINCIPLE

3

If you are dating someone pretty seriously, you'll soon begin to wonder if you are "in love." It can be hard to tell whether it's the kind of love that might end in marriage. You may grow closer and closer, only to be jilted or dropped. Or maybe you will be the one who feels it is necessary to bring an end to the dating relationship.

It is important to determine whether your relationship is "puppy love" or "true love." But before getting into the difference, let me say something that may surprise you: *Even if you truly love a person, it is not always reason enough to get married!* I point this out because a loving person may truly love many people. Marriage, however, includes many other considerations.

A BIG DIFFERENCE

When you feel you are "in love," it is difficult to sort out whether it's "puppy love" or "true love" because your emotions are so strong. Therefore, it is wise to listen to family or close friends who have your best interests at heart. They can be much more objective. They may see things your feelings prevent you from seeing.

Consider this description of true love from I Corinthians 13:4-7, TLB: "Love is very patient and kind, never jealous or envious, never boastful or proud, never haughty or selfish or rude. Love does not demand its own way. It is not irritable or touchy. It does not hold grudges and will hardly even notice when others do it wrong. It is never glad about injustice, but rejoices whenever truth wins out. If you love someone you will be loyal to him no matter what the cost. You will always believe in him, always expect the best of him, and always stand your ground in defending him."

THE DEMANDS OF PUPPY LOVE

There is a huge difference between puppy love and true love. When the captain of the football team and the head cheerleader start dating, they begin by experiencing puppy love. The cheerleader sees the football captain as a steady date so she no longer has to worry about being asked out every Friday night. She sees him as a "hunk" to parade around with, arm in arm. He makes a good senior prom picture, and all the other girls are envious because he's the catch of the class. She doesn't consider, "Do I meet his needs?" Instead it's, "Does he meet my need for a good date, a good image, and a good time?"

The captain of the football team thinks much the same way. He doesn't want go through the awkward act of asking a girl for a date every Friday night and risk an embarrassing "turndown." He wants to date someone who looks good in order to prove he can get "anyone he wants." He is not necessarily thinking, "How can I meet the needs of this young woman? How can I make her feel more confident in herself? How can I help her grow into the potential she has?" His concerns are more, "Does she make me feel good? Does she meet my needs? Does she make me look good in public and with my friends?"

These two feel physically warm and loving toward each other, but don't yet have any concept of true love. They are experiencing puppy love, but as Billy Graham has said, "Puppy love sure feels real to the puppy." The feeling may be so strong that they decide it's time to get married.

Let's look at the same couple a year later. She's pregnant and feels tired all the time. She hasn't fixed her hair or makeup for days. She is no longer the life of the party. Consequently, the guy "falls out of love" with her. But he's not in much better shape. The big football scholarship he was counting on for college fell through when he injured his knee in the last game of the season. He's working as a part-time mechanic at the local garage. He comes home dirty, smelly, and looking much older. He starts spending more time with his buddies, drinking and running around. He is no longer the attractive, charming, football hero. He feels like a "worn-out husband," and the ex-cheerleader also "falls out of love."

Various versions of this story are experienced thousands of times every year in our country. When puppy love is mistaken for true love, the results are not usually very pretty.

THE NATURE OF TRUE LOVE

When you truly love someone, you constantly ask yourself, "How can I help this person succeed? How can I help him look good? How can I help her develop all the potential she has?"

True love never includes negative kidding (where the winner is the person who makes the other feel worse). True love looks for ways to build, encourage, and make the other person feel more confident. True love is considerate. A person who truly loves you will go out of his or her way to meet your needs. If you don't feel that way about someone, you don't truly love that person.

In a counseling session a 46-year-old client told me, "Bobb, after hearing you explain the difference between puppy love and true love, I have to admit I have never truly loved my wife in our whole 22 years of marriage. My biggest question has been, 'How can she help me?' I'm embarrassed to say I have never once asked how I can help her." He broke down and wept. Then he continued, "For 22 years I have used my wife, and probably abused my wife . . . but I have never truly loved my wife. From now on I'm going to do everything I can to truly love her."

Two years later we talked again about their relationship. He told me, "These have been the best two years of our lives. I have tried nearly every day to do something to show my wife that I truly love her."

In your own relationships—especially romantic ones—make sure you understand the difference between puppy love and true love. With only puppy love as a foundation, it's only a matter of time before one or both people feel they have "fallen out of love."

27

One word of caution: Be careful to avoid unhealthy relationships where you give of yourself endlessly to meet your partner's needs, but the other person seems content to simply use you and never try to meet *your* needs. If you find yourself in this kind of one-way relationship, be aware that it may never change. You need to ask yourself, "Am I willing to settle for being used by this person for the rest of my life, or do I need to break off the relationship?"

On the other hand, you may be in a situation where the person you're dating truly loves you, but you see the relationship more as puppy love or friendship. It's important for you to discuss with your partner any major differences in your perceptions. You want to grow in the relationship at equal levels rather than one person becoming much more deeply committed than the other.

True love demands honesty. Don't settle for less in your family, dating, and marriage relationships.

KEY QUESTIONS

1. *Have you ever experienced puppy love? Have you ever experienced true love?*

2. *Is your current dating relationship closer to puppy love or true love?*

3. *How do your parents and close friends feel about your current relationship(s)?*

ACTION POINT

Who is one person you want to truly love? It could be a parent, brother, sister, grandparent, or possibly someone you're dating. In the next 30 days, make a point to go out of your way to express love as defined in I Corinthians 13.

"In the very important area of choosing a lifemate, it is essential to remember that more marriages end as a result of disagreement about money than any other single reason."

PRINCIPLE

4

ROBERT L. SNYDER—VICE PRESIDENT

T. J. RANEY AND SONS, INC., LITTLE ROCK, ARKANSAS

"You spent way too much money for that."
"I didn't realize before we were married how stingy you are."
"If only you made as much money as Jane's husband does!"

Cruel, bitter words like these ring off the walls of a lot of newlywed apartments. At this point in your life, you may not be staying awake nights thinking about whom you are going to marry. But there will come a time in your life when you wrestle with the decision, "Should I marry this person?"

At that point, a very important area of discussion should be, "Do we have a common understanding of money?" As Bob Snyder points out, "More marriages end as a result of disagreement about money than any other single reason."

Let me suggest a book called *Preventing Divorce* (Multnomah Press) that covers many areas to discuss with your future mate. It helps uncover any hidden assumptions you are making that might lead to divorce after you're married.

One section focuses on financial questions. For example, if you get married and things are "tight" financially, you may assume that all your income should go only toward necessities and paying bills. But your spouse might consider a new outfit or going to a movie a "necessity." If you weren't aware of such differences before marriage, they can cause tension and arguments until you work out how to handle them.

If nothing else, it would be helpful for your future mate to read through the financial section of *this* book. Then you two will have a common language and understanding of the assumptions you make about money. You can agree or disagree about principles such as not going into debt unnecessarily, not risking money you can't afford to lose, and so forth.

Mike Carter, an attorney in Oklahoma City, has seen many couples struggle in their first years of marriage, and he offers this bit of additional advice: "When you are first married, operate on a cash basis (without credit) until both of you have firmly established spending habits well within a defined budget which is updated annually."

KEY QUESTIONS

1. *What are the most important assumptions you make about money that you would want your future mate to make as well?*
2. *How do you plan to go about finding out how your mate thinks about money?*
3. *How important do you feel money is—even in the dating relationships you have?*

ACTION POINT

If you are dating regularly, spend at least half an hour during the next week or two discussing some of the financial principles in this book.

"In your early years of making money, live as frugally as possible in order that you may invest as much as possible."

DR. R. C. SPROUL—CHAIRMAN

LIGONIER MINISTRIES, ORLANDO, FLORIDA

As you begin living on your own—especially if you have marriage in mind—it is important to learn to make the most of sales, used things, and bargains. Remember, every dollar you let go through your fingers is a dollar you could have invested in a savings account to earn more money for you.

SAVINGS ADD UP

Let's say you're buying a car and have $1000 to spend. You see a car you like at that price, but there is another one you like almost as well—in excellent mechanical condition—for $500. If you buy the $500 car and put the other $500 in a savings account, you can still get around and have half of your money making more money!

This may seem like an obvious fact when you are talking about $1000. But it may not seem so obvious when you're talking about $10, $15, or maybe even $100. If you can buy a sweater for $30 that's almost as nice as a $130 one, you can still look great and put $100 into an investment.

Another way to look at it is that you can dress twice as nice for half the price. If you like fine clothes, wait until they go on sale and buy them for the same price that other people would pay during the regular season for less stylish clothes. Or find outlets that sell at a discounted price.

Of course, this principle applies to every other kind of item you buy. If by the time you leave home you have saved several thousand

31

dollars through frugal purchasing, you will have a nice savings account as you look ahead to marriage and family concerns.

Eating out is one real drain on your money, since you can eat much more economically at home. It is also wise to cut out grocery coupons, especially at places where they offer double coupon discounts.

A real motivator might be to set up a separate bank account where you put all the money you save. Think about a major savings account accumulated by buying generic products instead of brand names, or eating at home rather than eating out. Over a period of several years, you can put a lot of dollars in the bank. At some point, you will have enough to place a down payment on a house, buy a car, take a trip to Europe, or do something you really enjoy.

HOW WILL THIS APPLY WHEN I'M ON MY OWN?

In adulthood, you will make more major purchases (refrigerators, stereos, cars, athletic equipment, etc.). If you take time to look around a little, you can get some of these items for about half the price. You might find them at a garage sale or in a classified ad in the paper. Or you can wait until they are on sale. One of the reasons so many couples struggle financially is that they spend much more than necessary by paying full price rather than looking for bargains.

KEY QUESTIONS

1. *Where can you buy quality goods at discount prices?*
2. *Who do you know who might know where to get things on sale?*
3. *What are the best savings opportunities each year when clothes or various items go on sale (such as just after Christmas)?*

ACTION POINT

Make it a hobby during the next 30 days to buy everything you can at a reduced rate. Look for bargains, sales, a different supplier, or a store that might have a cheaper price. Make a game of spending as little as possible for the same quality items, and put the rest in your savings account.

Encouragement brings hope for the future. Specialize in being an encourager.

Each of us needs all the encouragement we can possibly get! Any comment that lessens the amount of hope for the future is discouraging. Comments that brings hope for a brighter future are encouraging. And there is no better place to practice being an encourager than among your family members.

ENCOURAGEMENT IS HOPE

Encouragement provides additional courage to a person by helping him or her take another step, go another mile, or start over again. He or she maintains that all-important hope. On the other hand, when people are *dis*couraged, their courage fails. They find it difficult to keep going.

Everyone enjoys being around an encourager. We like to be optimistic about the future. We appreciate people who bring new options, new possibilities, and new thoughts about how to reach the goals we've set for ourselves. We tend to shun discouragers.

Try it and see. If you tend to be negative toward a brother, sister, or parent, do just the opposite for a week or so. Is there a difference? More than likely, that person will respond favorably to your encouragement.

There are countless ways to bring encouragement to other people. Over your lifetime, learn all the ways you can to encourage people in any given situation. Someday you may be needed to bring encouragement where there is none.

SPECIALIZE IN BEING AN ENCOURAGER!

Young people aren't the only ones who get discouraged. Adults get discouraged, too. We all need help, and we can all give help to each other. There are no limits to the number of people you can encourage. When you see your parents getting discouraged—wondering if they're going to be able to make the mortgage payment, or if they're going to make it in a new job—become their encourager. Help them see hope for the future. Assure them they're going to make it. In short, encourage them!

KEY QUESTIONS

1. *Of all your friends, who most needs encouragement today? How can you bring hope to that person's future within the next day or so? (Be specific.)*

2. *Who among your family members (grandparents, parents, brothers and sisters, nieces and nephews) needs encouragement? How can you encourage them this week?*

3. *Who is the best encourager you know? How does he or she encourage you? Does this person's encouragement relate to his or her popularity?*

ACTION POINT

Make a list of the three people you know who most need encouragement. Provide some of that encouragement for them within the next seven days.

People need encouragement and instruction more than criticism.

PRINCIPLE

7

Principle #6 dealt with the importance of encouragement, but the topic is important enough for a second, related principle. It's one thing to neglect to encourage others. But even worse is to respond with criticism *instead of* encouragement.

PEOPLE NEED ENCOURAGEMENT

Think of times when you have been the victim of thoughtless words and unnecessary criticism. What good did it do you? None! People need encouragement and instruction far more than criticism. Encouragement provides hope. Criticism destroys it.

Encouragement is to people what gasoline is to a car. Without gas the car won't run, and without encouragement, people don't do so well either!

Specialize in being an encourager. Start at home, and start by eliminating critical remarks from your conversations. Realize that everyone needs hope and encouragement—parents, teachers, and friends. Tell them when they do good jobs. Assure them that things will work out. Help them see a brighter future. Encourage them!

PEOPLE NEED INSTRUCTION

One of the most trustworthy statements you'll ever hear is: "Nobody wants to fail; they just don't know how to succeed." When you see a younger brother, sister, or friend doing something incorrectly, don't criticize the person. Rather, ask yourself, "Does he

35

really *want* to do it wrong? Is she trying to fail?" Of course not! The person just doesn't know how to do it right. Perhaps all he or she needs is a little instruction.

The same goes for you. When you feel like you're failing at something because you don't know how to do it, tell your parent(s), "I don't know how to do this. I need some instruction. Could you help me?"

ELIMINATE CRITICISM

Anyone can criticize someone else. It's easy. It's simple. It requires no special skill. But it's just as easy and a lot more rewarding to encourage and instruct.

Continual criticism is one of the fastest ways to lose friends, discourage family members, and bring down all the people around you. No one likes to be around a person who is constantly negative and pointing out faults. Avoid this habit at all costs!

KEY QUESTIONS

1. *How do you feel when someone criticizes you?*
2. *How do you feel when someone encourages you?*
3. *In what area has someone been criticizing you where you simply need instruction?*

ACTION POINT

Think of a family member you would like to see win in life, and for the next 30 days try an experiment. Encourage that person in everything you see him or her do right. See how the person begins to respond. At the end of 30 days, I think you'll be pleasantly surprised!

"All miscommunications are the result of differing assumptions."

Dr. Jerry Ballard

8

"I thought you meant the front door, not the back door."
"I thought you meant the grocery store, not the mall."
"I thought you meant Jerry Bach. I called Jerry Ballard."

Miscommunications cause frustration, pressure, and tension! People can get angry, irritated, frustrated, and upset when someone else does the wrong thing, spends too much money, meets at the wrong place, or perhaps doesn't show up at all!

Once you get together with the other person and talk about how the misunderstanding happened, it usually turns out that each of you had made a different assumption.

ALL MISCOMMUNICATION?

When Dr. Jerry Ballard first told me this principle, I couldn't believe my ears! It seemed too simple to come from someone who was getting his Ph.D. in communications from Syracuse University. I said, "Jerry, I can't believe that someone as smart as you are would make such a general statement as this . . . saying that *all* miscommunications are the result of differing assumptions."

So for about three years I tried to find an exception—but never did! And for the last seven years I have been passing along this principle to other people.

One of the skills you need to master in life is the art of communicating clearly. You want to be able to "say what you mean, and mean what you say." Learn to become very specific when it comes to things like where to meet, how much to spend, and so forth. You will find that whenever there is miscommunication, you can trace it back to differing assumptions every single time.

OOPS!

As an adult, you will need to become more and more precise in your communications. Whenever you experience miscommunication with someone, the two of you may want to sit down and make clear your assumptions (what each of you believe to be true). Discover how your assumptions differed from the other person's. Then you'll know how to avoid this kind of problem in the future.

Imagine that a girl is getting ready for a date. She's expecting a young man named Tom to pick her up at 7:00 for a party. The doorbell rings, and there stand three young men, with three corsages, and each thinks he is her date for the evening. How could such a thing have happened?

Well, at school she had told her friends, "I decided to go to the party with Tom. When you see him after school, would you mind telling him I'll be ready at 7:00?"

One of her friends assumed she meant Tom Johnson; another assumed she meant Tom Oakey; and a third assumed she meant Tom Thompson. So each of them arranged for "Tom" to pick her up at 7:00. That's how all three showed up on her doorstep at 7:00! How embarrassing!

THE FAMILY APPLICATION

Think of how many family miscommunications arise because your assumptions are different from those of your parents. (According to this principle, I would guess *all* of them.) Be sure you are clear to explain your intentions to your parents. And if they don't make things clear to you, ask questions until you have clarified what they expect of you. It will avoid a lot of hard feelings (and perhaps some "consequences" such as grounding, scolding, etc.). After you become good at communicating with your parents and family members, relating well in other relationships comes very naturally.

KEY QUESTIONS

1. *Do a lot of people misunderstand what you're trying to say to them?*

2. *Are you upset with anyone right now over a misunderstanding of some kind? If so, what assumptions were the two of you making that were different?*

3. *What assumptions could you discuss with your parents to reduce the amount of frustration you feel with them?*

ACTION POINT

Think of a recent time when you miscommunicated to a family member and experienced a lot of frustration, pressure, or tension. What were you assuming, and what was he or she assuming? Discuss how your assumptions differed, and determine what you can do to keep that from happening again in the future.

PRINCIPLE

9

"Love people and use things. Don't love things and use people."

ART DeMOSS

How many times have you felt like an unimportant tool to be used by your boss? Maybe you've felt that if you did something less than perfect you'd be fired—thrown away like a rusty, broken wrench. Some adults are so driven by the desire for wealth and success, they end up using people rather than caring about them as individuals.

As you grow into adulthood, keep your heart focused on this principle of loving people instead of using them. Art DeMoss was the president of a large insurance firm that had several hundred employees and made hundreds of millions of dollars. Yet, according to his close friend, Bill Bright (founder and president of Campus Crusade for Christ), DeMoss always lived up to his own principle. He was a man who loved people and used things. He never loved things and used people.

LOVE PEOPLE

It's easy to take parents and family members for granted. But anyone you live with is a person who needs to be developed, encouraged, and loved. No one wants to fail. If someone isn't doing the best job possible, maybe that person just doesn't know how to succeed.

Three key words will help you deal with people in difficult situations: *care*, *honest*, and *fair*. An example of how you might use these words is: "Dad, I *care* too much about you not to be *honest* with you. In all *fairness* to the rest of the family, I need to tell you we wish you would spend more time with us."

Whenever you have bad news to share, these three words will help. Later on they will be useful if you need to tell people they are fired or that they're not going to get the raise or the position they want. "Sam, I care too much about you not to be honest. In all fairness to the rest of the group, Tom and Sandy have outperformed you by a long way. I care about you too much not to tell you personally that you're not going to get the position." Even in giving bad news you can communicate that you do care for a person and aren't just using him or her as a tool to accomplish what you want done.

DON'T LOVE THINGS

When people want a new car, house, job, company, or title too badly, they can get so focused on those things that they begin to see others simply as tools for their use. They take advantage of people to get from where they are to where they want to go. Never get so excited about having things that you run over people—especially parents or family members. Don't take advantage of people to get more things.

It may be difficult to find positive models who demonstrate the proper concern for people. If most of the adults you know tend to use people, keep looking until you find someone who really cares. Then follow that person's example.

KEY QUESTIONS

1. *When you plan events or work on a project, do you care for people and use things? Or do you love things and use people?*
2. *How do you feel when you're being used by someone?*
3. *Who do you know who truly loves people and uses things?*

ACTION POINT

Think of someone in your family who appears to be more interested in helping people than in simply reaching his own goals. Tell that person how much you admire his example. It will be encouraging to him or her, and the person may also provide additional thoughts on how to build people up instead of using them.

41

PRINCIPLE

10

"Don't overlook old people. Here is wisdom and experience for our asking. Here, also, is a group to whom we must give kindness and affection."

DR. JOHN R. MOTT

It's my guess that if you're reading this book, you already understand the value of gathering information from various sources. And you probably already know you can look to older people for wisdom and experience. It's a wise person who can learn from other people's mistakes rather than make all those mistakes personally.

A SOURCE OF WISDOM AND EXPERIENCE
As a young person with lots of energy and friends, it's easy to overlook older people. But don't forget; they were young once. They had the same kind of energy you have now.

Parents, grandparents, and older relatives are valuable sources of information. Get good at asking them to share what they have learned. Ask questions like:

- What advice would you give a young person today?
- What three principles have helped you most in life?
- If you were my age, what would you do differently?
- What did you do right in life?
- What single thing would you recommend I pay most attention to in life?

If you ask these five questions of each older person you meet, beginning with your family members, your life will be many times richer. Many older people have had experiences that could save you a lot of hard knocks. Learn from their mistakes. Ask hard-knock-saving questions like:

- What mistakes have you made in life?
- What lessons have you learned?
- What would you do over if you could?
- What should I avoid in life?
- What three experiences taught you the most about being a successful person?

Asking questions like these will give you tremendous insight you might miss completely if you ignore older people.

SHOW KINDNESS AND AFFECTION

One of the privileges I had as a teenager was growing up in a family with all four grandparents plus two great-grandparents still living. Though I spent time talking to and asking them questions, in looking back I wish I had spent more time with each of them. Now they are gone, and I can't sit and talk with them any longer.

While my grandparents were living, I always tried to show them kindness and affection. I went out of my way to help them when I could. I appreciated what they did for me—and for other people. I recognized their need for love and told them how much I loved them. I always tried to demonstrate how much they meant to me with a hug or a kiss. Go out of your way to be kind and affectionate to your own grandparents . . . and other older people.

HOW WILL THIS APPLY WHEN I'M ON MY OWN?

As a teenager it's important to relate with and care about older people. Most of the ones you know now are probably relatives. But as you get older, you'll discover how wonderful it is to have adults ten or twenty years older than you as friends and advisers.

As a way of remembering and respecting the feelings of older people, I often read the following poem. I first heard Gloria Gaither read it at a concert. I had tears rolling down my cheeks as I thought of older people I had known.

When I read this poem I'm reminded that someday I, too, will be old. What I have taught my children about relating to older people is the way they will treat me. What you teach your own children is the way they will care about you.

God, my hands are old.
I've never said that out loud before
but they are. I was so proud of them once.
They were soft
like the velvet smoothness of a
firm, ripe peach.
Now the softness is more like
worn out sheets
or withered leaves.
When did these slender, graceful hands
become gnarled, shrunken claws?
When, God?
They lie here in my lap;
naked reminders of this worn out
body that has served me too well.

How long has it been since someone
touched me?
Twenty years?
Twenty years I've been a widow.
Respected.
Smiled at.
But never touched.
Never held so close that loneliness
was blotted out.

I remember how my mother used to hold
me, God.
When I was hurt in spirit or flesh,
she would gather me close,
stroke my silky hair,
and caress my back with her warm
hands. Oh God, I'm so lonely!

I remember the first boy who ever
kissed me.
We were both so new at that!

44

The taste of young lips and popcorn,
the feeling inside of mysteries to come.

I remember Hank and the babies.
How else can I remember them
but together?
For out of the fumbling, awkward attempts
of new lovers came the babies.
And, as they grew, so did our love.
And, God, Hank didn't seem to mind
if my body thickened and faded a little.
He still loved it
and touched it.
And we didn't mind if we were no longer beautiful.
And it felt so good.
And the children hugged me a lot.
Oh God, I'm lonely!

God, why didn't we raise the kids
to be silly and affectionate
as well as dignified and proper?
You see, they do their duty.
They drive up in their fine cars.
They come to my room
to pay their respects.
They chatter brightly and reminisce.
But they don't touch me.
They call me Mom, or Mother or Grandma.
Never Minnie.
My mother called me Minnie.
So did my friends.
Hank called me Minnie, too.
But they're gone.
And so is Minnie.
Only Grandma is here.
And God, she is lonely!

MINNIE REMEMBERS from MIND SONG by Donna Swanson. Reprint by
permission only, Williamsport, Indiana 47993

KEY QUESTIONS

1. *What older people should you go out of your way to care about?*
2. *What questions could you ask them to help unlock their wisdom and experience?*
3. *How can you show each of these people kindness during the next week or month? (Write a letter? Bake cookies? Stop by for a visit? Telephone to say hello?)*

ACTION POINT

Do at least one extraordinarily good thing for each of the older people on your list within the next 30 days.

FINANCIAL

PRINCIPLES

"When investing money, seek advice from those who have expertise in the area of your investment. Pay generously for that counsel. Scrutinize carefully advice from those who are selling."

Lee Eaton

President, Eaton Farms, Incorporated, Lexington, Kentucky

The older you grow, the more you will be faced with the questions of how much, when, and where to make investments. (For the purposes of this book, we define "investment" as putting time, energy, or money into something in order to receive some benefit.) So let's take a closer look at the advice provided by this principle.

ASK THE EXPERTS

One of the easiest ways to lose money is to invest in something you don't know much about. Don't invest anything unless you know the field very well or have a friend who is an expert. And even when you are investing on the advice of a friend, go much more cautiously than if you know the area yourself.

For example, let's say you want to invest $2000 in a used VW and you don't know a lot about cars. You would want to have a trusted mechanic examine the car. Ask: "If I bought this car, how much repair do you think it would need immediately, and how much within six months?" Then add those estimated costs to the price of the car to see if you still feel it is a wise investment. Also ask the mechanic: "If you were in my position, would you buy this car? Why or why not?"

Some other times to ask for advice would include:

- Before you choose a school, ask the opinions of people who are actually going there.
- Before you buy a musical instrument, check with music

49

teachers or people who have a similar instrument.

- Before you buy a Walkman, television, radio, amplifier, etc., talk with someone who is really familiar with the item (other than the salesman) to get advice. Or take time to research the product and become an expert yourself!
- Before you choose a summer camp, make sure you talk to people who have attended.
- Before you invest your time in a class, check with people who have already attended to see if it was worthwhile.

This starter list gives you a feel for the kinds of situations where you may need to check with someone before investing. You'll add many other points over the years.

YOU GET WHAT YOU PAY FOR

As you move on into adulthood, you may pay a lot of money for advice on investments. For example, let's go back to the used VW. When you go to the mechanic, he may charge you $40 for a complete check of the car you are considering.

Because of the advice, you may decide not to buy the car. You've paid what seems like a lot of money without anything to show for it. Yet that $40 might have prevented a $2000 or $3000 mistake.

The older you get, the more you'll pay for advice. Don't think free advice is a bargain. Be willing to pay generously when people can provide expert advice. It is one of life's wisest investments in the end!

FIND PEOPLE YOU CAN TRUST

Anyone selling something obviously wants you to buy it so he can make money from the sale. In many cases (though not always) the salesperson is more concerned with the sale than with your best interest. Listen carefully to what a salesperson tells you, but also be sure to check with your advisers. Find a way to make sure the person is telling you the truth about key points.

I hate to make you suspicious by saying, "Don't trust salespeople." Some are completely honest, but others will shade the truth or tell white lies. And some will downright deceive you to convince you

50

to buy what they are selling. Good advice from trusted friends can counteract a lot of high-pressure salespeople.

HOW WILL THIS APPLY WHEN I'M ON MY OWN?
Lee Eaton, who provided this principle, has bought and sold millions of dollars worth of thoroughbred horses during the past 20 or 30 years. He has paid thousands of dollars for wise counsel, and has benefited a great deal from it. He has learned that you need to check out what some salesmen are saying to keep from getting "suckered" into a deal.

A common experience of adulthood is when a young newlywed couple gets approached by people selling vacuum cleaners, crystal, pots and pans, or insurance, and are asked to make a commitment of several hundred dollars on time payments. The couple naturally want to make their own decisions, and the salespeople may laugh if they want to check with "Mommy and Daddy." But if they don't check with someone, it is easy to get burned!

If you don't want to ask your mother and father for advice on investments after you get married, decide what favorite relative or friend you *would* feel comfortable asking. Don't make a major decision without asking at least two or three people for their perspectives. Otherwise, you will end up overpaying for a lot of stuff or end up kicking yourself because you made a bad decision!

All people make a certain number of bad decisions, so don't be afraid to take action. Just remember that asking at least three advisers can save you a lot of "egg on the face" moments.

KEY QUESTIONS
1. *What is the largest investment you will probably make in the next one to five years?*
2. *Who are the three people whose business judgment you would trust the most to help you with that investment?*
3. *Where have you seen your parents or friends make unwise choices because of not asking advisers their perspectives on investments?*

ACTION POINT

In the next 30 days or so, talk to your top three most respected financial advisers (parents, relatives, friends, or experts). Ask them what decisions they have made in the past on which they wish they had received counsel. Then see if they would be open to giving you counsel on financial decisions. Ask if in the future you could consult them for advice about any investment over $100 or $200.

"Know what it costs you to live, and live within your means."

DENNIS R. JAMES
PRESIDENT, JAMES FINANCIAL SERVICES, INC.,
LITTLE ROCK, ARKANSAS

From time to time everyone feels confused about how much he or she should spend on something. One of the best cures for feeling "out of control" financially is to "know what it costs you to live, and live within your means." In other words, you need to make a simple budget.

KNOW THE COSTS

Unless you have a system to anticipate all monthly bills, you may spend what you think is left over. Then you get caught without any money when a "surprise" bill comes later in the month.

It's easy to list all the areas where you spend money on a monthly basis. You can do this even if you only receive an allowance to use for lunch, movies, etc. Create a basic budget something like the chart on the next page.

As you can see, down the left-hand side you simply list the areas of spending and income, with each month across the top. Then you can look ahead through the year and say, "How much will I receive and spend in each of these categories during the next three months?"

When you check the difference (at the bottom) you can predict which months you'll be able to put money in the bank and when you may need to take some out. Some months you are not going to have enough income and will need to take some of your savings.

Know what it costs to live!

	January	February	March	April
INCOME				
Allowance				
Baby-sitting				
Other				
TOTAL INCOME				
EXPENSES				
Clothes				
Movies/Entertainment				
Lunch				
School supplies				
TOTAL EXPENSES				

Amount left over:
(Income minus Expenses)

DON'T SPEND WHAT YOU DON'T HAVE

A lot of people are embarrassed to say they can't afford something. Lloyd Murray, a TWA pilot, advises, "Practice saying, 'I can't afford it.'"

Get good at telling people right up front that you can't afford something. There are many, many things in life that we'd like to do, are wonderful to do, or would be helpful to other people, but sometimes we simply cannot afford to do them. If you don't have the money, don't spend it!

HOW WILL THIS APPLY WHEN I'M ON MY OWN?

Today, many adults spend more than they make. They end up having to put things on credit cards, which puts them further in debt. Interest begins to be added to the debt they already have, and soon they feel like, "We're never going to get out of this debt."

The best way to avoid debt is to "Know what it costs you to live, and live within your means."

54

KEY QUESTIONS

1. *What are all of your income sources for the year, projected out on a monthly basis?*
2. *What are all the categories in which you spend money in a year which could be listed down the left-hand side of the budget sheet?*
3. *What surplus or debt will you have at the end of the year if you simply follow your budget as projected?*

ACTION POINT

Put together a budget for yourself for the coming year. Make a commitment to sit down on the first of each month and ask, "How am I doing? Where did I spend too much? What am I doing with my reserves? Did I make as much as I thought?" In short, "What is it costing me to live? And am I living within my income?"

"Borrow only for things that will increase in value. It is a losing battle to borrow for things that depreciate in value (for example, cars, furniture, clothing, and vacations)."

DR. ROBERT C. ANDRINGA
PRESIDENT, CEO SERVICES, DENVER, COLORADO

Have you ever known anyone who regularly complained: "I think I'm in over my head. I'm not sure I'm even going to be able to pay back what I owe. Where am I ever going to get the money? I can't sleep well at night because of all the bills I've got to pay!"

You may not be losing sleep because of the heavy debt you've accumulated. I hope not! But if you find yourself in the position of continually "needing" to borrow money, I would strongly urge you to not borrow any more and to pay back what you owe. *Learn to save the money you earn until you can pay cash for what you want!*

BEWARE OF BORROWING

If you use credit cards, think of them like a checking account. Be absolutely sure money is available to pay the bill in full when it comes at the end of the month.

Our country has been described as "the land of easy credit." It's easy to borrow money and hard to pay it back. It's simple to charge something on a credit card, but difficult to find money at the end of the month to pay the bill. It becomes necessary to pay a few dollars and let the rest continue unpaid until next month. The problem is, each month you wait, the bill gets even higher because of interest.

Listen to how strongly George Underwood III, President of Underwood Development Corporation, feels about borrowing:

(1) NEVER, NEVER, NEVER borrow money to buy a

depreciating asset (charge cards, car, boat, TV, etc.).

(2) Borrow money to buy a capital asset only if you could still pay back the loan should the asset disappear from the face of the earth.

(3) Never ever borrow to buy any personal luxury item that "you just can't live without." Interest can work strongly for you or against you.

A MATTER OF INTEREST

Interest on savings can earn money for you, but interest charges on borrowed money can accumulate even though you aren't spending any money! The basic way interest works is like this: You ask someone to loan you $200. He says, "OK, I'll loan you that $200 for a year, then you have to pay me back plus interest of 10 percent" ($20 on the $200).

Now, let's imagine that at the end of one year you aren't able to pay back the $220. The person might say to you, "Well, I don't need the money, so 'let it ride' for another year." So in two years, you owe $220, plus 10 percent interest, or an extra $22 on that money. You now owe $242 to pay back the original $200. Let's say it goes a third year. Interest of $24 has to be added. You are now up to $266 to repay the person who loaned you the money three years earlier.

Compound interest requires that you pay back the money plus interest, and you pay interest on interest. Over the years, "interest on interest" can accumulate to the point where a $200 loan could cost you $300 or $400. It gets discouraging when you have borrowed money and each year you become responsible for the principle (the $200 you borrowed), the interest, *and* the interest on interest. Avoid borrowing if at all possible!

Yet compound interest can also work to your favor. If you put $200 in a savings account which pays 10 percent, at the end of three years you have $266 thanks to accumulated interest. If you don't withdraw any of it, you will eventually double your money.

You can determine how long it takes money to double by dividing 72 percent by the interest rate. The resulting number tells you how many years it will take to double the investment. For example, if interest is 10 percent, the formula is .72 ÷ .10, or 7.2. Your money will double in 7.2 years. With an interest rate of 20 percent, you could double your money in 3.6 years (.72 ÷ .20).

COMPOUNDING THE SITUATION
You work hard to earn your money, so why not spend it on something other than interest? The obvious conclusion is, avoid debt whenever possible! The following story illustrates the effects of the compounding factor:

It is said that the man who invented the game of chess was asked by the king what he would like as a reward for giving the king such a delightful game. Being a mathematician, the man said, "Oh, King, it pleases me greatly that you enjoy the game of chess, so let me ask a simple request. Take the chessboard and put one kernel of wheat on the first square. On the second square put two kernels of wheat, on the third place four kernels, on the fourth square put eight, on the next sixteen, on the next 32 kernels, and so forth. Simply keep doubling it for the 64 squares on your chessboard." The king responded, "Oh, that's easy; it shall be done!"

However, the king hadn't figured the effect of such compounding. By the time he got to the final square, millions of bushels of wheat would have accumulated. Learn to let interest compound *for* you instead of *against* you!

Verley Sangster is the national urban director for Young Life in Denver, Colorado, and father of eight children. Any father of eight knows financial pressures. Listen to his experienced counsel:

"Always maintain an excellent credit rating. Working to keep your credit good first of all makes you live within your means. That relieves you of the stress and anxiety of wondering how to pay for things. A good credit rating also provides a tremendous amount of security, knowing that there is a line of credit you could draw on if needed (for example, for a medical emergency)."

If you don't borrow money, you may not be able to get the newest car, a high-fashion wardrobe, or the newest trends in whatever you're buying. But you can be assured that you'll never go bankrupt, either.

Dennis James is a successful C.P.A. (certified public accountant) in Little Rock, Arkansas. Dennis has consulted with some very, very rich people over the past 15 years. Seriously think about his wise advice about credit:

"Avoid entering into debt. I will not be so extreme as to say never get into debt, but there are actually very few times when debt is appropriate. I have personally concluded that the only debt which I will have is the mortgage on my residence, and I will scrutinize and manage it very carefully. To appreciate this you must know that three years ago I had over $750,000 of debt related to investments. I have both experienced and repeatedly witnessed the intense pressures that result from living with debt. Even in our universities you will be told that leveraging or using other people's money is a smart thing to do. Don't believe it. Living with debt will rob you of your sleep, your smile, and your serenity."

Usually, in order to pay off official loans or money borrowed from a friend, you must spend less and make more—reduce expenses and increase income. If you pay back money that you have borrowed ahead of time, people will appreciate it. Your credit then stays A+ for future extreme emergencies when you have absolutely no option but to borrow.

KEY QUESTIONS
1. *How much have I borrowed altogether?*
2. *How can I pay that back as quickly as possible?*
3. *How can I keep from ever going into debt again?*

ACTION POINT
If you have already borrowed money and are feeling pressure to pay it all back, don't borrow any more. Pay back what you have borrowed as soon as possible. Don't make the pressure worse by borrowing more.

"You can't win 'em all. You will have financial discouragements, setbacks, and disappointments, but . . . this phrase will help you over the rough places of your life."

ROBERT L. BIEHL (MY FATHER)

MANCELONA, MICHIGAN

By now you have probably experienced some financial disappointments. The stereo you bought at a garage sale disappointed you when the cassette player didn't work. You thought your new bike was going to last forever, but soon it was scratched and scraped and needed to be replaced. You thought the small investment you made would make a lot of money, yet nothing has happened so far.

It seems that many people think they will never fail as they "steam full speed ahead" in life. Most people assume that life is easy. They act as though they have been promised wealth and prosperity.

The reality, however, is that life is difficult and unpredictable. Very few people are born with "a silver spoon in their mouths."

YOU CAN'T WIN 'EM ALL

The good news is that you will have financial success at many points in life. You'll have a savings account. You'll likely make more than you earn by wise money management. You may invest and the stock will go up. If you buy a house, the value is likely to increase.

But if you are expecting life to be consistently easy, you are setting yourself up to be disillusioned. You will do much better to assume that life is tough and that you are going to lose some as well as win some. Then when disappointments come, you won't be devastated by them.

For example, life may be going very smoothly for you; you have a little extra money in savings and are dreaming about how you'd like to spend it. Then, just when you least expect it, your car overheats and you have to replace the radiator. There goes your extra "fun" money! You will be able to keep from getting too depressed, however, if you remember that life isn't out to get you. These things sometimes "just happen," and you were fortunate to have the extra money to pay for it.

At the same time, don't develop a casual attitude toward risk. If faced with a decision that could cost your home or financial security, never think to yourself, *Well, I can't win 'em all, so if I lose this one, I won't worry much about it.* Maintain a healthy perspective toward risk and potential loss at all times.

One final reminder from Samuel W. (Sam) Miller, president of Pioneer State Mutual Income Company, Flint, Michigan:

"There have been times when inwardly I have said to God, 'Why did You let me make that awful move?' The answer always comes back: '*You never asked Me!*' I strongly encourage you to simply *ask Him!*"

KEY QUESTIONS

1. *What has been the most financially disappointing thing in your life so far?*
2. *How did you feel when that disappointment came?*
3. *Would it have helped if you had understood that "you can't win 'em all" rather than feeling like life was supposed to be perfect?*

ACTION POINT

Ask your parents or financial advisers to tell you a story or two about an investment that turned bad on them, and what lessons they learned from the experience. Discuss how even the most careful planning sometimes ends in disappointment. Ask them if they agree with the statement, "You can't win 'em all!"

PRINCIPLE

15

"Don't spend money you don't have."

JOHN ERWIN—PASTOR TO STUDENTS AND FAMILIES

GRACE CHURCH, EDINA, MINNESOTA

Have you ever heard anyone say, "Let's just put this purchase on the credit card. We'll figure out how to pay for it later"?

Anytime you think about spending money you don't have, a red light should flash in your head that says, "Warning! Warning! Warning!" If everyone would follow this principle, there would be no bankruptcies, no debt pressures, fewer sleepless nights, no business for loan sharks, and no "highway robbery" interest rates. In short, life would be much easier.

DISCIPLINARY ACTION

My son J. relates to this need for financial discipline. He says that after receiving his paycheck, his friends often encourage him to go skiing or join them in some other activity. But since that money is needed to pay bills, he usually has to refuse. Otherwise he would be left with an expensive memory and no money left for groceries!

Discipline is saying no to something you want *now* in order to have something of a higher value you will want *later*. John Erwin, the source of this principle, is a friend and youth pastor who has worked with a lot of teenagers and young married couples. Here is his additional advice about discipline in regard to money:

"Don't spend what you don't have. So many young people are lured into the easy credit nightmare because of impulsive buying. Installment purchases are usually based on the wrong assumptions. In our credit-conscious age, we have been led to believe that there are no consequences to impulsiveness. However, we will reap what we sow, especially interest rates (18 percent or more on credit cards, etc.). It takes discipline to make money and buy what you need, not what you want."

When you're young, you may equate *discipline* with "punishment." But now you need to think of discipline as a positive adjective to use in describing yourself. ("I'm disciplined.") Discipline can enable you to accomplish your financial goals and reap the benefits.

Philip Artz has the right perspective or. financial discipline: "I am not a financial wizard; just a hardworking person from 'down on the farm' in Ohio. My first advice is discipline, discipline, and more discipline."

KEY QUESTIONS

1. When have you spent money that you didn't have?

2. How did you feel about it?

3. What were the consequences of that spending?

ACTION POINT

Probably every adult alive has a horror story to tell about spending money he or she didn't have. Ask your parents to be open and tell you about a time when they spent money that they shouldn't have. Ask what lessons they've learned in the process . . . and what advice they would have for you in this area.

PRINCIPLE

16

"When investing for future equity appreciation, always look for location and path of progress!"

LARRY MUNSON—PRESIDENT

MUNSON PROPERTIES, FOUNTAIN VALLEY, CALIFORNIA

Imagine for a minute that you are married. You have one child and have been living in an apartment for two and a half years. The apartment is beginning to seem smaller and smaller as your child gets bigger and bigger. You just learned that your first child will soon have a baby brother or sister!

Work has been good, so you begin the exciting and frustrating process of looking for a small home of your own. You agree as a couple that you don't want a town house or condominium. You want a single family home, with a white picket fence and a small yard for the kids!

But where do you look? You contact your favorite real estate person and start looking at homes. But the real estate agent uses some of the most confusing terms:

> Principle,
> Interest,
> Appreciation,
> Equity,
> Points,
> Down payment,
> Wraparound loan.

Soon you just want to go home, turn on the TV, and rest your feet and brain. When this happens to you, remember Larry Munson's advice, which has proven trustworthy over years of successful real estate investing: "When investing for future equity

64

appreciation, always look for location and path of progress!"

Let's take this wise advice and chew on it piece by piece.

INVESTING

Yes, your home is actually an investment—not like stocks and bonds, but still an investment. You put in money and over the years your home hopefully becomes more valuable. But if you see a house *only* as an investment, when it goes up in value you may be tempted to sell at a high price and move. Don't forget it is also your home.

Our family has lived in several homes over the last 25 years. We have done well in California residential real estate. We have bought and sold houses, making money each time. We have lived 10 years in our current house and plan to stay here for a long time. We are happy that the house has gone up in value, but we don't plan to sell. This is our home.

Perhaps you will move several times before you retire. If you do, you will see your home as an investment, so it is important to make money each time you move. To be able to make money on a house, you have to buy at the right price and in the right location. Not all houses are great investments that go up in value!

FUTURE EQUITY APPRECIATION

Equity is the amount of money you would have left in your pocket if you sold your home and paid off the mortgage. For example:

House Value	$100,000
Mortgage	$ 60,000
Equity	$ 40,000

Appreciation simply means increase in value. If you buy a house for $100,000 and sell it for $150,000, during the years you owned the house it appreciated in value $50,000.

LOCATION

A wise old gentleman once said, "There are three keys to choosing great real estate: (1) Location! (2) Location! (3) Location!"

Let's say the house you are considering is located in a great part of town in a housing tract with 100 other houses. What will make your house more attractive than all the others to the person who buys it from you?

If five of the houses have a better view, they have a better location. They will likely appreciate and sell faster. So choose the best part of town you can afford. Location adds value.

PATH OF PROGRESS

Choose a house where there is a lot of building going on. The more people moving into an area, the greater the likelihood you can get an appreciated (increased value) price when you sell.

You may not buy a house for the next ten or more years. But when you do, remember this principle!

KEY QUESTIONS

1. *Where is the path of progress in your area? Where are the new homes being built?*
2. *How much has your home appreciated since you moved in? Ask your parents.*
3. *When do you plan to start saving for a down payment on a house?*

ACTION POINT

Go buy a house. (Just kidding!)

Talk to anyone you know in real estate and ask where he or she sees the best house buy in your area. Have the person explain why! You may be surprised by the answers, and the other person will be surprised at your question.

"People who make money extremely fast usually lose it or spend it all. People who make money over a longer period of time tend to keep it."

DAVID M. HARMON—SENIOR VICE PRESIDENT

SOUTHWEST LUBBOCK NATIONAL BANK, LUBBOCK, TEXAS

There are stories that would make a grown person cry about how quickly people go through inheritances or unexpected monies they have received. Most people are used to dealing with money on a monthly basis, but not in a lump sum. Therefore, when they get an inheritance or legal settlement, win the lottery, win prizes on a game show, collect insurance, etc., they often do not know how to handle the money.

If you should get a lump sum of money from any source, may I suggest six things:

1. Seek the counsel of a trusted accountant. You may actually receive substantially less than you anticipate due to taxes, etc.

2. Give your tithe (a percentage) to God—to the church or other worthy causes.

3. Put some of the money into a secure savings program you can't touch for at least a year. Friends will come around wanting to borrow for a wide variety of "harebrained schemes." You need to be able to tell them, "I'm sorry, the money is tied up and I can't get to it for a while." This gives you time to evaluate what would be the wisest course of action to take with your money.

4. Pay off any long-term indebtedness you may have (such as a car) so that your monthly payments are reduced.

5. Put a substantial sum in a very safe, secure, long-term investment—maybe for college or the down payment on a house. Let the interest compound and work for you.

6. Take whatever is left over and put it into high-risk investments or spend it on things you want to buy. But avoid spending all your money on high-risk investments or "fun money" before you make the previous investments.

Two of my son's friends inherited money—one 50 grand and the other 40 grand. They each paid cash for a new car, which will be worth nothing in 30 years. Then they got nice apartments, paying $800 a month rent, and all kinds of fancy furniture, credit cards, etc. With 40 grand they think, *I don't even have to work anymore! I'll just live off that.* If you are fortunate enough to receive a large lump sum of money, don't make the mistake of letting it all get away from you. Make sure you can benefit from the gift years from now as well.

KEY QUESTIONS

1. *What would you do if you inherited $20,000 today?*
2. *What if you couldn't spend any of it on yourself for the next six months? What would you do with it then?*
3. *Do you know of anyone who has inherited money or come into large amounts of money and lost it?*

ACTION POINT

Go talk to a few people who have unexpectedly come into a large sum of money. Ask them about the lessons they've learned.

"It is extremely difficult to make your fortune in a salaried position. . . . If you want to make a real fortune, you have to come up with a product, idea, or service that is in demand or required by the masses."

18

BOB BATTERBEE
BATTERBEE'S ANTIQUES AND COLLECTIBLES, BELLAIRE, MICHIGAN

If your dreams and ambitions for financial success are far above the average, then Bob Batterbee's counsel to you is very wise. It is extremely difficult to make a fortune on a salary. Even with a salary of $100,000 a year, it's still not likely that you'll have your own private jet and limousine. To actually "hobnob with the rich and famous," you need to develop an idea, product, or service that is demanded or required by a lot of people.

Think of something that is wanted or needed by every one. Then find a way to get it to them at an affordable price, but in a way that you will still make an honest profit. If you can do this, the chances of becoming superwealthy are greatly increased.

A WORD OF WARNING

Yet as you start out, be aware that most ideas turn out to be pipe dreams. About 80 percent of the businesses which start in America fail within the first five years. Even good ideas can fail for want of follow-through, adequate money, or a wide variety of other reasons.

If you want to be superrich someday, the first thing you need to do is get a steady job. You can then pay the bills and still be able to have some time in the evenings to work on your idea, product, service, invention, etc. Then when your idea begins to make money and you have enough savings to pay six months' worth of bills, you can quit your steady job and begin working full-time on your idea!

In starting a company, one problem is that you have several fixed expenses (salaries, rent, telephone, lights, heat, etc.), but a variable income. Some months you have a lot of income and other months you don't have much at all. As a result, you can go into debt very quickly.

LUNCH BREAK
Are you the kind of person who would like to be superrich someday? If so, one of the best things I can recommend is to find a few people who have made a lot of money in an honest way. Invest a few of your dollars in buying them lunch. Ask how they became successful and what they could teach you about what they learned in the process. See if they would advise you as you begin to develop your own business over the years.

As a teenager or young adult, it is very easy to fall into the trap of assuming an older person will pay for lunch. When you call the person you have chosen, tell him you insist on paying for lunch at his favorite place. Say clearly that you want to talk about how to make and manage money. When you meet:

1. Do not let the other person pay for lunch.

2. Be prepared to ask good questions. Have a list of of 10 to 15 ready to ask. For example, your list might include:

- What are the three most important principles you've learned in making and managing money?
- If you had it to do over, what would you do differently?
- If you had a chance to do it over again, would you stay on a secure salary, or would you start a company?
- What are five to ten keys for making a business really successful?
- What would you do today if you were my age?

3. Take careful notes when you're with the person, and possibly even record the conversation (with permission).

4. Always follow up with a thank-you note expressing how much you appreciate the person's time to help you win in life.

At your age, $30 for a lunch may seem like a waste of baby-sitting or lawn-mowing money—especially when the other person makes 100 times what you make. But this lunch may be the wisest investment of $30 you'll ever make in your life. If you wanted to hire this person as a consultant, you might have to pay $500 to $5000 an hour for his time. But when you go out to lunch, the person will probably be happy to share with you his finest thoughts.

He or she will also be impressed with your ingenuity, drive, and maturity. If it makes sense to do so after your conversation, you may even ask if the person knows of a job opening. Say that you are looking for a job where you can learn principles like you have been discussing. Who knows? You may just get a job offer on the spot!

KEY QUESTIONS

1. *How much money do you really want to have someday?*
2. *Are you willing to pay the price of the risk and uncertainty of income in order start a company where you would make a lot of money?*
3. *Who are the three most successful people you know who have developed their own companies and make a lot of money?*

ACTION POINT

If you decide that someday you would like to be "superrich," decide on the one person you admire most in terms of moneymaking ability. Set aside $20 to $30 of your own money. Call the person on the phone and ask if you can take him or her to lunch.

"Never turn down anything that's free."

LLOYD MURRAY

TWA PILOT, ST. LOUIS, MISSOURI

Every so often in life you are offered something valuable that is free. Take it while it's available and decide later if you want it!

I'll never forget one night when I was 16 while I was working on my uncle's turkey farm. He became upset with one of the turkeys and threw something at it. To his great surprise, his aim was better than he expected. He hit the turkey in exactly the wrong place on its head and it dropped over, dead. My uncle, getting madder by the minute, took the turkey and angrily threw it out into the cold, snowy night. I asked him what he was going to do with it, and he said, "I've got a a freezer full of turkeys now; I'm just going to leave it out there."

I asked him, "Do you mind if I take it home?"

He said, "Sure, go ahead." So when I got home that night, I woke my mom up and she dressed out about a 30-pound turkey. Our family had free turkey for a number of meals.

Of course, it is not every day that you are going to be offered a free turkey, or a free anything. But I have found wisdom in Lloyd Murray's quote, "Never turn down anything that's free!"

Sometimes you get something free and two days later you decide you don't want it. You don't want the junk any more than the person who gave it to you, so you just throw it away!

On the other hand, once you get something, you may find you can trade it to a friend for something you want more. For example, suppose someone gave you a basketball he didn't use anymore.

Even if you don't play basketball, you could trade that basketball to a friend for a soccer ball you *would* use. Financially speaking, the soccer ball would be just as free as the basketball was!

Never hesitate to ask a person, "What are you going to do with that? Are you just going to throw it away? Do you mind if I get that out of your trash? I think I could use that in my garage." Don't be embarrassed to ask for something if it looks like the person is simply going to discard it or throw it away. It can become valuable to you later on. (But never ask for something unless you are quite sure the other person is going to throw it away.)

At the same time, don't become a "pack rat." Every once in a while go through all your things and see what you no longer want or need—clothes, athletic equipment, magazines, etc. Instead of throwing these things out, see if you can trade with anyone. Frequently, you can exchange your unwanted items for something of far more value to you.

KEY QUESTIONS

1. *What have you ever gotten that was free?*
2. *Was it worth the effort?*
3. *How could you creatively go about getting free things from people in your neighborhood? (For example, going the last day of a garage sale and offering to take everything that's left.)*

ACTION POINT

Go through your things and make a pile of items you no longer need or want. Then see what you can trade with a friend. If you can't trade, simply give something to another person "free" and maybe suggest that they alert you when they are about to "clean house."

"Making money requires motivation. . . . Determine early what you want to use money for, and make that your goal. Never make your goal just money."

JOE KIMBEL

RETIRED MINISTER, LAGUNA HILLS, CALIFORNIA

As you set goals in your life, you'll find that most of them take money to accomplish. But you will soon find that a goal of making more and more money is far less motivating than a goal to do something specific with the money.

Peter Ochs, president of Fieldstone Corporation in Newport Beach, California, puts it this way: "Money is never the goal. It is always a by-product; and if it becomes a goal, you have lost your focus." His is a very meaningful quote, especially coming from a man who builds several million dollars' worth of homes every year.

WHY DO YOU WANT MONEY?

It seems that adults frequently get sidetracked where making money is concerned, until sooner or later they make money just to make more money. Before long the amount of money they have begins to shape how they value themselves and other people. In short, money becomes the end rather than the means. It is distorted thinking to consider yourself better than someone else because you have more money than that person. Yet when money becomes someone's sole focus, such thinking often takes place.

Make sure you think of money as a means, not an end. (See Principle #23.) Set goals that your money can help your achieve, but don't let money itself be the goal. These principles are just as important in adulthood as they are before you leave home.

KEY QUESTIONS

1. *What goals do you have for the next 30 to 90 days?*
2. *How much money will those goals take?*
3. *How can you go about earning the money to reach the goals you've set?*

ACTION POINT

Write down the top three things you would like to do in the next 90 days. Determine how much money you would need to make in order to reach those goals.

PRINCIPLE

21

"Investigate and gather as much information about an investment as possible. Remember nothing is free (financially) despite what anyone tells you."

TIMOTHY S. SAMBRANO—PRESIDENT
LSI FINANCIAL GROUP, IRVINE, CALIFORNIA

Before buying something or investing money, be sure to get plenty of information. What information will you need? Perhaps the basic questions from Rudyard Kipling are the best starting place for gathering facts: "Who? What? When? Where? and Why?"

Who?—Who is selling? Who is trying to get you to invest? Can you trust the people involved? What's their background? Have they been in business for a while? Do they really know what they're talking about? Are they people you'd like to do business with over time? Have you checked them out with the Better Business Bureau?

What?—What features are you looking for? What guarantees are involved? What payment schedule is expected? What benefits will you get? What difference will this purchase or investment make?

When?—When do you need it? When will it go on sale? When will the guarantee expire? When do you expect it to break down?

Where?—Where will I need to pick it up? Where will I put it when I get it?

Why?—Why do I want it? Why do I want this particular one? Why am I getting it from this store? Why do I believe this sales-person? Why do I feel a need to get it today instead of waiting?

How?—How will I get it? How will I pay for it? How will it be put together? How will it fit with the rest of my things? How will it be delivered?

How much?—How much will it cost totally? What will the monthly payments be? How much will the interest rate be? How much are the late fees? How much are the prepayment penalties?

These are just a few questions to help you gather the information you need to make wise decisions about things you buy. Not all of these questions will apply for every purchase. But when you are making a big decision, ask yourself these questions first. Just because you want something doesn't mean it is a good or wise thing to buy. Get the facts.

HOW WILL THIS APPLY WHEN I'M ON MY OWN?

Before you leave home, probably the largest purchases or investments you make will be things like a used car, a college education, a stereo, snow skis, or similar items. However, when you get older you may find yourself buying a condominium, house, country club membership, new automobile, airplane, boat, or mountain cabin. Or you may invest hundreds of thousands of dollars in stocks, bonds, real estate, etc. The older you get, and the more money you have, the more important this principle becomes.

Always get the facts! When you think you have enough information, you may still want to check with two or three financial advisers. Tell them what you've found out and ask what other information they would try to get before buying the item you're considering. Make decisions based on solid information!

KEY QUESTIONS

1. *What are you planning to buy or invest during the next few weeks or months that will represent a lot of money to you?*
2. *What facts do you need to know before deciding?*
3. *Can you think of a time in the past when you have bought or invested in something, only to wish you had gotten more information first?*

ACTION POINT

Do specific research on the next "major" purchase or investment you are going to make, and ask yourself all the questions listed earlier in this chapter. See what information you can dig up that will help you make a wise purchase or investment.

PRINCIPLE

22

"How much in? How much out? When? More return is better than less. Sooner is better than later. Simple is better than complex. 'For sure' is better than 'Maybe.'"

MAYNARD MUNGER

REAL ESTATE AND INVESTMENTS EXPERT, PLEASANT HILLS, CALIFORNIA

In the future when you are asked to invest money in something, you will need to ask a few questions to help you find the right kind of investment. There are thousands of questions you could ask, but the above guidelines are good ones to memorize and begin with.

HOW MUCH IN? HOW MUCH OUT? WHEN?

Probably the most fundamental questions you can ask about an investment are, "How much do I put in? How much will I get out? How much is guaranteed? How much is speculation? When will I get the payoff?"

Until the person can answer those questions for you, don't put one red cent into his proposal. Especially watch out for tentative phrases such as, "hope so . . . probably . . . sure looks good" and other similar uncertain terms.

MORE RETURN IS BETTER THAN LESS

Obviously, the more return you get, the better the investment is. Compare investment opportunities. If you put in an identical amount but get more back from one than the other, the greater return is obviously a better deal, all other things being equal.

Incidentally, this would be a good place to quote what Dr. Ted Engstrom, President Emeritus of World Vision, Inc., always advises, "Never decide from an option of one. If you have only an option of one, you have no decision. Decide from at least two alternatives."

Whenever you look at an investment opportunity, you may want to ask yourself, "If I didn't have this investment but still needed a place to put my money, where would I put it?" Then you always have an option of at least two. For example, you could put it in a savings account or certificate of deposit, both of which are less risky. You should always have an alternative to the investment you are considering.

SOONER IS BETTER THAN LATER
Seth Rohrer, president of Church Growth Services in South Bend, Indiana, says that with any investment he wants to see his personal dollars come back to him within two years and then be making money beyond that. He considers any investment with a return longer than two years as less than ideal.

SIMPLE IS BETTER THAN COMPLEX
When an investment is too confusing to clearly understand, it is too complex. You want to put your money in investments that are simple enough to be understood completely.

The older you get, the better you will be able to understand complex opportunities. But no matter how old you get, avoid investing in things you don't understand. Complex opportunities can be a setup for someone to take advantage of you.

"FOR SURE" IS BETTER THAN "MAYBE"
Over your lifetime, you will be offered many opportunities to invest in things that may happen . . . where the possibilities are good . . . that will probably work. Some such investments will offer an enormous percentage of return. The risk is higher, but if it works you get your money back plus a high return on that money. But beware, because the more risk, and the higher percentage of possible return on your investment, the less likely is the guarantee that you'll get your money back if it *doesn't* work.

If you are in a position where losing the money wouldn't hurt at all, go ahead and take a higher risk. But if losing the money would cause financial problems, stay away from the "maybes" and stay with the "for sures." Of all the money you have, only invest the percentage you can afford to lose in the risky areas, and put the money you can't afford to lose in safer areas such as banks and certificates of deposit.

HOW WILL THIS APPLY WHEN I'M ON MY OWN?
It goes without saying that the larger your investments are, the more important these assumptions become. If you are investing $1000, the questions you ask may not be nearly as important as if you are investing $10 million. But at any level of investing money, these are important principles to memorize and keep in mind.

KEY QUESTIONS
1. If you are about to make an investment of some kind, answer the three questions, "How much in? How much out? When?"
2. Compare the investment you are considering with simply putting the money in a certificate of deposit. Ask the same questions and see which investment turns out better.
3. Have you ever lost money in an investment? If so, how did you feel, and how could these questions or assumptions have protected you?

ACTION POINT
Ask your parents if they have ever invested in something that didn't turn out exactly like they thought. Ask them how this principle might have kept them from making the mistake that they made.

"Money is a means, not an end."

TAPIO AALTONEN—PRESIDENT

THE PEOPLE'S BIBLE SOCIETY FOUNDATION, VIVAMO, FINLAND

PRINCIPLE

23

You've probably heard of people who wanted to be so rich that someday they could go into a bank vault, strip naked, and roll in $20 bills. There is supposedly a true story of one man who actually had himself buried in cash money because he loved it so much.

WHAT MONEY CAN AND CAN'T DO

Kalevi Lehtinen, an international evangelist on staff with Campus Crusade for Christ says: "Money has no other value than what people give it. You can't eat it; you can't drink it; it can't give you love or warmth; you can't take it with you when you die."

Money can buy you food; it can buy you drink. It can provide for and protect those you love. You can give it to the church or God's work and store up treasures for yourself in heaven. But money in itself, as an end—money for money's sake—is not something to invest your life in. Unless you can decide what you want to do with money, money itself isn't of much value.

Dr. Bill Bright, founder of Campus Crusade for Christ, says: "Always make money your servant, not your master. I have many friends, even Christians, who are consumed by material things. They own homes, yachts, airplanes, and all kinds of material possessions, which in fact result in their being servants of their possessions. Some of them are always trying to justify owning another plane or another house, and they are uncomfortable because they know it is not good stewardship. They invite their friends to enjoy with them whatever they have, and it seems to me as I observe, that they wear themselves out trying to justify their possessions. They become servants instead of masters of their wealth. So do not be overly impressed with material possessions."

Dr. Ted Engstrom, President Emeritus of World Vision, Inc., says: "Money/wealth is in no way evil. It is only when we 'love money' that we grieve God, according to His Word."

Mark Petersburg, director of the Christian Embassy in Washington, D.C., says: "Hold all you have with a loose grip. Albert Schweitzer said, 'If you own something you cannot give away, you don't own it; it owns you!'"

Great men and women have said it many different ways, but the bottom line is the same. Don't fall in love with money. Don't give money too high a value in your life. Consider it simply a way of getting the things that are important to you.

Money is a means by which you can choose what you like to do. Becoming rich doesn't mean that you don't have to get up at 6:30 A.M. to go to work. Instead, it gives you a reason to get up and work at something you are excited about doing.

HOW WILL THIS APPLY WHEN I'M ON MY OWN?

Adults sometimes get caught in the trap of making more and more money. The more they have, the more they want. There never seems to be a point at which they are satisfied.

A lot of adults feel that having more money will someday make them "happy." But the definition of happiness I like is: "The feeling you get when you have what you want and want what you have."

Getting more and more things you want will not guarantee happiness. The secret lies in wanting what you have. For example, you may want three new sweaters, but you don't have to be unhappy until you get them. If you focus your attention on the 30 sweaters you *do* have in your closet, you'll probably find your happiness factor increasing a great deal.

If you find yourself unhappy, concentrate on what you have that you really want, rather than what you want and don't have. You'll find your happiness level begin to grow.

KEY QUESTIONS

1. How would you complete this sentence: "To me, money is
   _____."

2. Do you think of money more as a means or an end?

3. Have you ever met anyone who seemed to want money for money's
   sake? If so, what were your honest impressions of that person?

ACTION POINT

Identify the richest person you know personally. Contact the person (without saying that you have concluded he or she is the richest person you know) and ask, "What does the phrase, 'Make money a means, not an end,' mean to you? Do you believe this is wise advice? Have you ever known anyone who made money an end, not a means?"

I think you will find this conversation a particularly interesting one!

"When you are thinking of making any investment, take twenty-four hours to 'sleep on it.' Think about the investment nonemotionally."

ROBERT D. SMULLIN—PRESIDENT

DAY FOCUS, SAN JUAN CAPISTRANO, CALIFORNIA

How many times in your life have you made a quick decision to buy something you wanted desperately, and then the next day you wished you hadn't? We've all done it. The tendency begins at about the age of ten, and even with age it doesn't get any easier to say "no."

That is why Bob Smullin's advice is so wise and helpful. When you take twenty-four hours to think about major purchases, the chances of making a wiser decision triple or quadruple.

WHY WAIT?

You will rarely miss out by waiting twenty-four hours. It is highly unlikely that the first purchase you consider is "one of a kind" or even the cheapest one. By considering other options during the twenty-four hours, you may avoid the disappointment that comes after making an impulsive purchase and finding out later you could have done better.

For example, you may be very excited about a specific car, and overlook a lot of obvious problems just because you want it so badly. Three weeks later the car may start to fall apart, and you will wish you had taken twenty-four hours to have a mechanic look it over.

A word of warning: Many salespeople will try "every trick in the book" to keep you from taking a day to think about your purchase. They know that anyone who thinks about something for at least twenty-four hours and gets past the emotional excitement of the moment tends to come back and renegotiate the price.

Just knowing this should give you a tremendous advantage when you are talking with salespeople. Don't be manipulated by their efforts to force you into a quick, impulsive decision.

One of the oldest ploys of a salesperson is the use of the word *limited*. Salespeople give the impression that the opportunity may not be here tomorrow. Another trick is implying that only a small number of people can purchase the item. Pressure is put on you to act now and not take any more time to think about it.

A TIME TO SLEEP; A TIME TO ACT
At the end of your life I hope you will be able to look back and say, "There were a few things I missed by not acting quickly enough. But I sure saved myself a lot of trouble by being patient. There were many situations I am thankful I did not jump into, because they didn't work out. The times when I was able to ask the right questions, get advice, and 'sleep on' the decision were the investments and purchases that turned out to be the wise ones."

In one sense, it is fair to say: "The more excited I am about an investment or purchase, the more I need to sleep on it." Simply letting some of the excitement and emotion dwindle out of an investment or purchase gives you a clearer head to look at the decision realistically.

Another bit of very sound advice on purchasing comes from Lloyd Murray, a seasoned world traveler, negotiator, art collector and wise buyer: "Never bring your checkbook when you're buying an expensive item. (This is relative—now maybe it's $100; in ten years it may be $1000.) This allows emotions to settle, removes the salesperson's influence, and lets you really examine the value and the need. 'Sleep on it,' then buy."

HOW WILL THIS APPLY WHEN I'M ON MY OWN?
Adults can get into the exact same trap that kids and young adults do. Many adults want something so badly that they get "suckered" into saying yes today rather than giving themselves twenty-four hours to think about it.

Start now to form the habit of resisting sales pressure by answering politely and firmly, "No, thank you. I will wait and think about it for at least twenty-four hours." Make this response a habit in your life. Don't get caught off guard by someone who is trying to talk you into fast decision making.

KEY QUESTIONS

1. *Have you ever experienced the sales pressure that people put on you to make a quick decision?*
2. *How have you coped with this situation in the past?*
3. *Have you ever gotten "suckered into things"? How did it feel?*

ACTION POINT

Ask your parents to explain a situation in which they got "suckered" into something and wished the day after that they had taken twenty-four hours to think about it. (You will make your share of mistakes, no matter how hard you try to avoid it. But one of the surest signs of wisdom is learning from other people's mistakes and not making the same ones yourself.)

A foolish person says, "I have to make my own mistakes." A wise one says, "I don't need to lose thousands of my dollars learning my own lessons; I'll learn from the mistakes of other people and keep my money." Of course, when you do make mistakes, they can provide a tremendous education if you learn from the experience.

"In purchasing anything (generally over $100), hear at least three salespeople tell their stories."

BOB TIEDE—MINISTRY DIRECTOR

JOSH MCDOWELL MINISTRY, DALLAS, TEXAS

25

Has a salesclerk ever promised you: "This is the best deal you'll find anywhere. You aren't going to beat this price. This is the best offer in town!" Whenever you hear these kinds of sales lines, they should act as mental triggers to remind you of Bob Tiede's principle.

Chances are, there are two or three other establishments in the area where you could get just as good a bargain, or possibly far better. Always have two or three options. As you compare, you may prefer to deal with one store versus the other. Perhaps one store's service department is superior. Or you may just prefer doing business at one place over the other. Why not shop, invest, and be involved where you enjoy it the most? Even when prices are the same, the value will vary as you factor in service, staff attitude, and your preference for shopping there!

You may be saying to yourself, "But there's only one 1957 Chevy two-door hardtop available that I've been able to find!" That may be very true. But if that car were not available, ask yourself what would you buy instead. Then see how the other car compares with the '57 Chevy.

HOW WILL THIS APPLY WHEN I'M ON MY OWN?

Adults have to deal on a regular basis with fairly large purchases, and maybe once or twice a year with *major* purchases (homes, cars, condominiums, and so forth). These purchases may cost hundreds, thousands, or even millions of dollars.

This principle is as applicable for any adult as it is for you during your young life. When choosing a summer cabin, for example, it is important to look at three or more of them before making a decision. Suppose a couple visits the first cabin and decides they would be very happy there the rest of their lives, so they buy it . . . but then friends visit two months later and tell them they could have gotten twice the space for half the money, or that another identical cabin was located in a community they would rather live in. The couple could spend the rest of their lives regretting the decision, or choose to make another costly move, simply because they didn't listen to at least three sales presentations before they finalized a major decision.

KEY QUESTIONS
1. *What are you going to buy soon that will cost over $100?*
2. *What are the three best sources of supply for that purchase?*
3. *Who are the people you know with the most sources or contacts that you could ask for help in finding a "better deal" somewhere else?*

ACTION POINT
Get your planned $100-plus purchase in mind. Then do a comparative study by filling out the chart below:

	Source 1	Source 2	Source 3
Price			
Shipping/Handling and Installation Charges			
Salesman (Rate 1 to 10—10 = best, 1 = terrible)			
Service Department (Rate 1 to 10)			

Which one would you prefer?

Compare the three sources for the item you are about to buy. I think this one experiment will give you a rich experience in comparative shopping, and I hope you'll see the value of using this principle for the rest of your life!

"Risk only what you can afford to lose."

R. MICHAEL CARTER

ATTORNEY FOR BOONE, SMITH,

DAVIS, AND HURST, TULSA, OKLAHOMA

"Let's go all or nothing."
"Let's bet the farm!"
"Tonight I'm going home rich or busted!"

These quotes may be overheard in a Las Vegas gambling casino, at a card game, or in a brokerage. They are exciting, but dangerous, attitudes.

People differ a great deal in what they consider risky. Some feel comfortable risking lots of money, time, or energy. Others are very cautious by nature. Whatever your attitude toward risk, this principle provides wise counsel for you, your friends, family, and life mate.

LEVELS OF RISK

Many financial opportunities include a certain amount of risk. Tom's proposed investment may require that you risk not getting back all your money. Joe's risk may not allow you to get back *any* money. Sam's risk may require additional money from you later. Bill's investment may risk money you don't even have now! Whenever you are considering a risk, remember: "Risk only what you can afford to lose."

"But," you may ask, "how much can I afford to lose? I don't really want to lose *any!*" The answer depends in part on how much you have. Just about anyone can afford to risk $5. It wouldn't bankrupt your life savings if you lost it. And if you're worth $500 million, you could probably afford to risk a million or two without being severely hurt if you didn't get it back.

Anytime you consider risking more than a month's income, a bright yellow light should go on. If the risk involves more than three to six months' income, the light should be bright red. And anytime you are risking an entire year's income, you are probably taking a risk you cannot afford. Your situation may be slightly different, but as a rule of thumb, these guidelines are appropriate.

Any opportunity that could potentially cause you to go bankrupt is far too great a risk.

THE WORST THAT COULD HAPPEN

Paul R. Schultheis, president of Real Properties Incorporated in Arcadia, California, is a major real estate developer and property owner in Southern California. He has been involved in millions of dollars' worth of real estate transactions over the past 20 years. Listen to his advice in relationship to risk:

"Always calculate the maximum downside potential of any deal or transaction that you enter into. If the downside, worst-case prospect could cause you to go into bankruptcy or severely hamper your ability to remain or continue in business, you should not get involved regardless of upside potential."

Ask yourself, *What is the worst thing that could possibly happen?* Could it cause you to go under? Then don't take the risk, no matter what you could gain if it works!

Incidentally, one helpful insight is that life's situations tend to break down into time, energy, and money. The more time you have, the less money it takes. The more money you have, the less time it takes. For example, let's say you had to move 20,000 gallons of water from one lake to another. If you had 20 years (a lot of time) to do it, one person could manage it (which would not take much energy). The only cost would be one person's salary for 20 years. On the other hand, let's say you had to move the water in one day. You would need to spend a lot more money to hire many additional people. You may need as many as 1000 people to carry 20 gallons each in that day. The more money you have, the less time things

91

normally take because you can hire people to get them done.

If you have borrowed some money, it is better to take two or three years to pay it back than to risk gambling on something with the possibility of bankruptcy. Frequently, people decide to gamble major money on the lottery, cards, or an athletic competition. They think, *If I can just hit the jackpot, I'll pay all my bills in one day.* Don't try to shorten the time too quickly. It is better to get the debt paid off for sure than to risk everything and lose.

HOW WILL THIS APPLY WHEN I'M ON MY OWN?

Sometimes people make decisions that risk their homes, businesses, cars, or material possessions, on a single opportunity. There may come a time in your adult life when you'll be tempted to do this.

You'll think about selling your car or putting a second or third mortgage on your house in order to put all that money into a glamour stock that is "sure to go from $80 to $800 a share overnight." But the realities of adult life are that most "sure things" turn out to be not only unsure, but disastrous. Whenever you are considering a major risk, remember Mike Carter's expert advice and "risk only what you can afford to lose!"

KEY QUESTIONS

1. *Are you thinking of taking a risk?*
2. *What would happen if you didn't take the risk at all?*
3. *Is there any way through information or advice that you can reduce the risk to a safer level?*

ACTION POINT

Sometime during the next month, ask one or two adults to tell you about the "sure things" in their lives that didn't work out. Learn from their mistakes rather than making the same ones yourself.

"Start saving money now. People think in order to save a lot of money, you have to make a lot of money. In reality, acquiring a substantial sum of money requires only two things: time, and the discipline to consistently work toward a goal."

JACK HANSLIK, JR., PUBLISHER, DANA POINT, CALIFORNIA

In addition to this principle, look at what Jack Hanslik, Jr. has to say about saving money: "The magic of compound interest takes effect when we start putting money away on a regular basis. For instance, if you start today to save $10 a month at 12 percent interest,

> in 20 years you will have $9,198;
> in 40 years, $97,930;
> in 60 years, $953,866;
> in 70 years, $2,964,860.

"On the other hand, you can see if you were to put $20 per month away, the principle of compound interest would not just double, but would dramatically increase proportionately through the same span of time. Time and consistency are the tools for you to become financially independent if you will simply follow these guidelines:

> (1) Establish a goal.
> (2) Decide on a plan.
> (3) Do it on a regular basis."

THE SECRET TO WEALTH

Over the years, I have had opportunities to interact with some very wealthy people. A major difference between people who struggle to get by and those who could be considered wealthy is one specific principle. Poor people live on their paychecks and save what's left (usually very little, if anything), and rich people put some in savings first and live on what's left.

That seems like such a simple principle, doesn't it? Put some into savings out of every paycheck, and live on what's left. Haven't you found already that you tend to live on what you have? If you have $10 in your pocket, you get by. If you have $100 in your pocket, you get by. Don't be shocked when I tell you that if you have $1000 in your pocket, you get by.

As Jack Hanslik, Jr. has shown us, if you start saving $10 a month with compound interest, over time it really makes a huge difference. Fortunately, one of the advantages of being young is that you have time on your side. Imagine being 60 and not having any retirement plan set up. Then imagine yourself 60 years from today after having saved only $10 a month at 12 percent interest—you would have $953,866 in the bank! That is nearly a million dollars you would have for retirement. If you put that sum in a bank at 10 percent interest, your income would be $90,000 a year for the rest of your life without ever having to use any of your savings. Time is on your side—start saving now.

J. Scott McBride, president of Marketing General, Inc., in Washington, D.C., advises you to think of your investment money as "seed corn." He says: "The farmer understands seed corn. Never invade your seed corn—always keep it invested and working for you." A farmer who eats his seed corn has nothing to plant, and will eventually become bankrupt.

HOW WILL THIS APPLY WHEN I'M ON MY OWN?

When it comes to money management, many adults think: "I'll pay all my bills; I'll give my money to the church; and if there's any left over, I'll take some for me." This is actually backward thinking. As a result, such people pay bills but end up in a position where nothing is ever left for investing or saving. They are stuck always working for money rather than letting their money work for them.

May I suggest that you form the habit of getting a paycheck and: (1) Giving God His share first; (2) Putting some of the money in your savings account; and (3) Living on the rest. If you form this habit now, later in your life you will be very thankful you did. In addition, you will always have a backup fund for emergencies.

Consider the advice of Dr. Bob Andringa, president of CEO Services in Denver, Colorado: "From the time you are young, give 10 percent of all you earn to the church and those in need . . . invest 10 percent and keep those investments earning dividends for you . . . live on what is left. If you do this, starting soon regardless of your income, you will have plenty to enjoy and share with others when you are older. I have tried to follow this. It works!"

KEY QUESTIONS

1. *How much do you think you could save each month without really hurting your budget? Do you think you could save $10? $20? $30?*
2. *At what age would you like to go to school, start a business, buy a house, or make some other major purchase or investment?*
3. *With compound interest, say at 10 percent to 12 percent, what amount of money could you have by the age you want to start your business?*

ACTION POINT

Fill out the following formula: Starting now, I plan to save $_____ per month. I can currently get approximately _____% interest compounded on my savings. It is my current plan to continue doing this for a period of _____ years, at which time I will be _____ years old, and I will have money available to _____.

Start now on a plan to put just $10 or $20 away per month (or per week, where it builds four times as fast). You end up with a tremendous amount of cash to start your own business, buy your first home, or bring to life whatever other dreams you have.

You may also want to check with some financial advisers and ask them how to go about finding the best return rate available on your money in the current money markets.

PRINCIPLE 28

"I have known many who could make money, but not many who could hang onto it. The people who can retain wealth once earned, and increase it, are the ones to observe."

KING A. CROW—CHAIRMAN AND CHIEF EXECUTIVE OFFICER

ARKANSAS FEDERAL SAVINGS BANK, LITTLE ROCK, ARKANSAS

What if you were fortunate enough to land a job tomorrow that paid $100,000 a year? It sounds good, but if your new lifestyle required $101,000 a year, in twelve months you'd be $1000 in the hole. You may say, "What an obvious statement!" But if you reduce the dollar figures, doesn't this situation describe a lot of people you know? The more they make, the more they spend; and before they know it they end up in the hole.

MAKE IT AND KEEP IT

Basically, there are three aspects to money:

     (1) Making income;

     (2) Controlling expenses to create cash reserve; and

     (3) Managing money to make more money.

There are some people who are great at making money, but not so good at controlling expenses. They always end up owing money, no matter how much they make. Then there are people who are great at controlling expenses. They can pinch a penny until Abe Lincoln cries "Uncle," but they don't know how to make money. As a result, they keep having to pinch pennies.

A key to success in your financial life is to make money and control your expenses so you have some left over at the end of each month. Then manage that money well by saving, investing wisely, and generally having that amount of money make more money for you. This is the key to actually accumulating wealth.

HOW WILL THIS APPLY WHEN I'M ON MY OWN?

Obviously, as you get older this principle still holds true. As the old saying goes, "If your outgo exceeds your income, your upkeep will be your downfall."

One of the keys to financial stability and accumulation of wealth is to have wise financial advisers. (See Principle #11.) These people can give you a good perspective at all points having to do with money. If you don't have financial advisers as an adult, you can make a lot of serious and costly mistakes. Let's say, for example, you do actually end up making $100,000 some year. A good financial adviser will help you make intelligent investments, pay all your required taxes, and use your money to its best advantage.

One of the first ways to maximize the use of your network of people is to ask your most trusted friends who they would recommend hiring as a financial adviser. I encourage you to have a financial adviser from the time you are 25 years old and beyond.

KEY QUESTIONS

1. *How much money have you actually made in the last five years (ballpark figure)?*
2. *How much money have you saved in the last five years?*
3. *How much money have you made off of your savings in the last five years?*

ACTION POINT

Remember who you identified as the wealthiest person you know (Principle 23, Action Point)? Contact that person again and ask, "What is your key to keeping money once you've made it?" The person will give you some good principles on how to keep money that you've made. Be sure to write them down and add them to the ones in this book.

PERSONAL

PRINCIPLES

PRINCIPLE

29

"One of the realities of life is that if you can't trust a person at all points, you can't truly trust him or her at any point."

CHERYL BIEHL

LAGUNA NIGUEL, CALIFORNIA

You may know the story of the time Abraham Lincoln bought something at a country store, and the clerk gave him two cents too much change. Young Abe didn't realize this until he had walked two and a half miles home. When he got home and put his change on the dresser, he noticed the extra two cents. Abe didn't just keep the money. He didn't pretend the change was right, or simply ignore it. He put the two cents back in his pocket, walked the two and a half miles to the store, returned the money, and walked home again . . . with a crystal-clear conscience.

HONESTY EARNS TRUST

In today's economy, two cents isn't nearly as much money as it was back then. But let's say the clerk at McDonald's gives you an extra two dollars (or twenty dollars) in change. When you find out, would you go out of your way to return it?

One of the realities of life is that if you cannot trust a person at *all* points, you cannot truly trust him at *any* point. Has a person ever lied to you? Deceived you? Stolen from you? After you found out, could you put all your trust in that person again?

Don't give anyone a reason to distrust you. Begin this habit while you're young, and maintain it when you're old. Be squeaky clean, totally honest, 100 percent pure in all your business dealings—especially when it comes to money management. Don't ever be dishonest! Develop a reputation that is above question.

Lloyd Murray, a friend and a TWA pilot, says he teaches his children that, "Honesty is like a box full of good things given us at birth. Each time we do something a little dishonest, something is taken out of the box and can never be replaced." If we permit ourselves little white lies, pretty soon we are dealing with gray lies, and eventually black lies.

BUT EVERYONE ELSE IS DOING IT . . .

Whenever you are tempted to be dishonest, go way out of your way to resist the temptation. Occasionally you may be tempted to steal something. "Friends are doing it, and they're not getting caught. The candy bar would taste good. The piece of clothing would fit comfortably under a coat." But again, stealing is dishonest.

If you're caught in a dishonest statement or action, it will put a major black mark on your reputation. It doesn't let you sleep well at night, and something is taken out of that little box of good things that can never be replaced. Even if no one ever found out, your conscience would still be a haunting voice telling you that you are a person who cannot really be trusted.

As a result of honesty, three things will happen.

You'll get a good reputation. As an honest person, your good reputation will grow. Listen to what my lawyer friend, Braydon W. Sparks, has to say about reputation: "Honesty pays. A good business reputation stands on many things, but the primary one is honesty. You'll have constant opportunities to be tested and approved in this area—often with money (yours and others'). Don't pass any of them up."

You can sleep at night. You can "rest easy" knowing that you haven't cheated anyone, and that no one is going to find any "skeletons in your closet." Your conscience is clear.

You can live with yourself during the daytime. When you look in the mirror you can say, "I am an honest person," which is an extremely valuable and affirming piece of information.

Lying, cheating, and stealing are all parts of the same thing: lack of honesty. Be honest in all things!

HOW WILL THIS APPLY WHEN I'M ON MY OWN?

The honesty principle isn't just for the growing-up years. Prisons are full of adults who felt they could lie, cheat, or steal, and "get away with it." They didn't!

The world is also full of people who have lied, cheated and stolen, and *have* "gotten away with it"—or so they think. They are not in jail. No one has ever caught them. But conscience hounds them day and night, reminding them that they are dishonest. Their sense of self-worth, self-confidence, and self-value is greatly reduced. They can't respect themselves. No matter how successful such people become, if in fact they have been dishonest in getting what they have, they will never be at peace. Honesty pays—in more ways than one.

KEY QUESTIONS

1. *Have you ever been dishonest with money?*
2. *What do you think would happen if you returned the money? What if you went to the person and agreed to pay for whatever you have taken? How would your conscience feel?*
3. *What difference do you think it will make with your conscience over a period of time if you simply choose to ignore the places in which you've been dishonest? How would it feel to go to bed tonight with a crystal-clear conscience?*

ACTION POINT

Make a commitment to yourself right now to correct anything you've done dishonestly. If you have lied, cheated, or stolen, do what you can to make it right today. Your conscience won't let you rest until these things have been cleared up. And if you have a "clean slate" before you leave home, you can enjoy living on your own all the more.

"We must deal with circumstances as they are, not as we wish they were. Failure is assured when we practice denial, when we refuse to face reality. Be absolutely ruthless with yourself with regard to recognizing, facing up to, and dealing with hard realities."

KING A. CROW—CHAIRMAN AND CHIEF EXECUTIVE OFFICER
ARKANSAS FEDERAL SAVINGS BANK, LITTLE ROCK, ARKANSAS

We human beings probably have 100 different ways of denying that something is wrong. Even when we know something isn't going to work, or when we're not going to be able to pay a bill, we put off facing reality. And we delay to the very last second telling someone if we're not going to be able to come through as we had promised.

ESCAPING REALITY

One way people try to escape those realities is to get drunk. Then they just have the problem *and* a hangover.

Another escape is to get high on drugs, but the drugs wear off and they're still facing the problem.

A third temporary escape is to tell the other person what he or she wants to hear, even though it is a lie. ("The check is in the mail." "I'll take care of it right away." "I already handled that." "They'll take care of you down at our branch office.")

And a fourth way some people handle problems is simply denial. ("It's no problem. . . . It will all work out. . . . Don't be concerned.")

FACING REALITY

Sometimes reality is difficult to face. But the longer you try to deny problems, the more overwhelming they become. On the other hand, when you are honest with people, they tend to understand.

One night I was flying from Detroit to Washington, D.C.

I happened to sit next to a gentleman who looked about 45 years old. He was wearing a tailored suit and shoes that must have cost at least $300. He looked like one of the most successful executives I had ever seen.

My eye caught the title of a paper he was studying, which was something to do with a Senate hearing. To make casual conversation, I asked him, "Are you a senator?"

He said, "Oh, no, I am a venture capitalist." (A venture capitalist is a person who puts cash into new ideas and businesses to get them started, in return for a percentage of the company.)

I asked him, "How do you decide whether or not to loan money to a person?"

He said, "We get literally hundreds of requests a month, and the way I decide is to find out how the person has dealt with failure in the past."

"What does that tell you?" I asked.

He replied, "Well, if business isn't going well, some people will avoid you or lie to you. Some will have someone on their staff talk to you. Some cross the street to avoid meeting you. Some deny that there's a problem. But others will call and tell you what the problem is, how it developed, why it developed, and what they are planning to do about it. They give you a new forecast as to when they feel the profit should be forthcoming."

He continued, "The first question I ask someone who wants to borrow money from me is, 'When have you failed in life?' If the person says, 'I've never failed,' I don't give him any money. New ventures are high risk, and if he fails I don't know how he'll handle it. But if he tells me about a failure, I can see if he faced the failure directly. I listen carefully to make sure he dealt with it as a responsible adult should. Then I check out the story. If it is true and the deal makes sense, I give the person the money!"

This story simply highlights the fact that people who deny problems are in for more problems. But others tend to understand and give breathing room to those of us who face problems in a realistic way.

KEY QUESTIONS

1. *What is the toughest issue you are dealing with today?*
2. *Are you facing it or denying it? Are you using alcohol, drugs, dishonesty, or denial to avoid dealing with it?*
3. *How can you move from denial to facing the issue realistically?*

ACTION POINT

Make a list of steps to help you solve your number one problem. If another person is involved, tell him or her what your plan is. Ask if it makes sense and request help, if appropriate, to deal with the reality you are facing.

"Your teachability will remain one of the bedrock issues for you to make the most of . . . making money and then in the management of that money after you have it."

DENNIS RANEY—NATIONAL DIRECTOR

FAMILY MINISTRIES, LITTLE ROCK, ARKANSAS

One of the greatest compliments you can pay to an adult is to ask for his or her advice, and then really listen to what the person has to say. Occasionally you might get some humorous counsel like you would find in country music songs, such as, "My advice to you, son, is younger women, faster horses, and more money!" Or, "The only things you can really trust in life are 'Old dogs and children and watermelon wine.' " But most people will give you the best advice they can. They want you to avoid making the same mistakes they have made.

LEARN TO BE TAUGHT
By reading this book, you already demonstrate wisdom and maturity. You are trying to learn from the advice that many people have contributed. It brings great pleasure when people see others take advantage of lessons they can pass along.

Unteachable people are in a sad position because they've learned all they're going to learn, they know all they're going to know, and basically, they are stunted for life. As long as you remain willing to ask people for help, you will continue to grow and develop the full potential you have as a person.

Ask questions in school or at work instead of waiting to be told what to do or how to do it. This keeps you involved and helps make sure you're doing things correctly. That's called learning!

Don Biehl, my uncle, has taught me, "Don't be afraid to ask

questions from anyone who is an expert at making or managing big money. Most people will gladly take time to tell you the highlights and pitfalls of their job or business. Their experiences could be very valuable to you in the coming years."

Set your goals high. You can become what you want to be—a doctor, lawyer, or anything else. But whatever you want to become, one of the real keys to succeeding is to be teachable.

One word of caution: Even if your goals are high, make sure they are achievable. Let's say, for example, as an adult you are five feet tall and you decide you want to train and become a member of the L.A. Lakers. You could take advice and practice *for the rest of your life*—and never make the team. So keep your goals realistic while you learn to be what you want to be.

KEY QUESTIONS

1. *Have you ever tried to teach someone who was a very eager learner, who wanted to learn everything he or she possibly could about the subject? How did that experience make you feel?*
2. *Have you ever tried to teach someone who simply wouldn't listen— who was unteachable? How did that experience make you feel?*
3. *Who is the person you would most like to learn from in life?*

ACTION POINT

Make a list of three questions you would like to ask the person you listed for question #3. What would you say if he or she came to you and said, "I'll teach you whatever you'd like to know. What would you like to learn from me?"

Make an appointment to visit the person if you possibly can. If you can't meet in person, write or call to ask for wisdom, perspective, and advice on your three questions. You may be very pleased with the response.

Throughout your lifetime, teachability is one of the finest qualities you can cultivate in yourself, your children, and your grandchildren!

"Hard work is critical. . . . Successful people . . . work harder than the others. It is not luck. It is not coincidence. It is not inheritance. It is not contacts. It is hard work!"

BO MITCHELL—PRESIDENT

EXECUTIVE NETWORK, DENVER, COLORADO

One of the things our society values most highly is work. We work to make money, to support our families, to buy things, to "make a living." Work is a very important activity.

Dennis Rainey, the national director of Family Ministries, in Little Rock, Arkansas, stresses the importance of good work: "Forget not the importance of faithful, hard work. We live in a culture that is looking for a quick fix and the instant buck. Make it your aim to work hard every day, and faithfully discharge your duties to the utmost of your abilities."

Solomon, the wisest man who ever lived, warned: " 'A little extra sleep, a little more slumber, a little folding of the hands to rest,' means that poverty will break in upon you suddenly like a robber, and violently like a bandit" (Proverbs 24:33, 34, TLB). In other words, "You snooze, you lose!"

Bo Mitchell adds, "It has always amused me that many people look at successful men and think, 'Look at that lucky man; he has it all going his way, and he never really had to dig for it.' What a joke!"

You may have heard the saying, "The harder I work, the luckier I get." I have found this to be true.

Dr. F. Carlton Booth, retired treasurer of World Vision International, a friend who is most enthusiastic about his work, gave me the following poem:

109

WORK
"A SONG OF TRIUMPH"

When Captain John Smith was made the leader of the colonists at Jamestown, Virginia, he discouraged the get-rich-quick seekers of gold by announcing flatly, "He who will not work shall not eat." This rule made Jamestown the first permanent English settlement in the New World. But work does more than lead to material success. It gives an outlet from sorrow, restrains wild desires, ripens and refines character, enables human beings to cooperate with God, and when well done, brings to life its consummate satisfaction. Every man is a Prince of Possibilities, but by work alone can he come into his Kingship.

Work!
Thank God for the might of it,
The ardor, the urge, the delight of it—
Work that springs from the heart's desire,
Setting the brain and the soul on fire—
Oh, what is so good as the heat of it,
And what is so glad as the beat of it,
And what is so kind as the stern command,
Challenging brain and heart and hand?

Work!
Thank God for the pride of it,
For the beautiful, conquering tide of it,
Sweeping the life in its furious flood,
Thrilling the arteries, cleansing the blood,
Mastering stupor and dull despair,
Moving the dreamer to do and dare.
Oh, what is so good as the urge of it,
And what is so glad as the surge of it,
And what is so strong as the summons deep,
Rousing the torpid soul from sleep!

Work!
Thank God for the pace of it,
For the terrible, keen, swift race of it;
Fiery steeds in full control,
Nostrils a-quiver to greet the goal.
Work, the Power that drives behind,
Guiding the purposes, taming the mind,
Holding the runaway wishes back,
Reining the will to one steady track,
Speeding the energies faster, faster,
Triumphing over disaster.
Oh, what is so good as the pain of it,
And what is so great as the gain of it?
And what is so kind as the cruel goad,
Forcing us on through the rugged road?

Work!
Thank God for the swing of it,
For the clamoring, hammering ring of it,
Passion and labor daily hurled
On the mighty anvils of the world.
Oh, what is so fierce as the flame of it?
And what is so huge as the aim of it?
Thundering on through dearth and doubt,
Calling the plan of the Maker out.
Work, the Titan; Work, the friend,
Shaping the earth to a glorious end,
Draining the swamps and blasting the hills,
Doing whatever the Spirit wills—
Rending a continent apart,
To answer the dream of the Master heart.
Thank God for a world where none may shirk.
Thank God for the splendor of work!

                                        (Angela Morgan)

111

I close with one last important dimension about work, pointed out by my friend Tom Raney, President of T. J. Raney and Sons, Inc., Little Rock, Arkansas, in quoting Dr. Scott Peck. He says, "Dr. Peck has an important chapter entitled 'Delaying Gratification.' If you will work hard and do what you know to be right, you will wake up someday and find yourself successful and respected by your peers. If you spend your life trying to hit a home run each day to be successful tomorrow, in all probability you will not succeed."

KEY QUESTIONS

1. *How do you feel about the work you do? Do you do it enthusiastically and with a special flair?*
2. *What pleasures do you get out of work besides money?*
3. *What "work" things do you enjoy so much you would do them even if no one paid you?*

ACTION POINT

Try an experiment. For the next three days at work, try being really excited about what you are doing. Look for ways to get involved, to encourage people, to compliment others, and to be positive about the work you're doing.

When you're bored, it's time to use your creativity rather than blaming someone else for your condition.

PRINCIPLE

33

Trying to have more fun is a national pastime! But, what is fun? How do you have more fun? Bumper stickers ask, "Are We Having Fun Yet?" TV commercials promise fun if we merely buy the right sports vehicle. Even with all the talk about fun, it may seem hard to identify or manufacture.

FUN: A DEFINITION

I define fun as *uninhibited spontaneity*. Think about the last time you really had fun. Could that time be described as *uninhibited*? You weren't restricted by money, time, social pressure, etc. You simply acted *spontaneously* and did whatever you wanted to do at that moment.

Another word which needs to be defined is the exact opposite of fun: *boring*. It can be defined as *inhibited and nonspontaneous*. Whenever we're bored we are inhibited by certain conditions: time, money, repetition, or parents who restrict what we do, say, or think. We feel "boxed in."

Is it possible to convert a boring activity—mowing the lawn, cleaning your room, washing dishes—into a fun experience? Yes, it is, with a little practice. First of all, use your creativity to change the situation. Think of brand-new ways of doing anything you've done a "zillion" times.

How can you clean your room in a way no one has ever considered? If you could figure that out, then cleaning your room (at least

113

that once) might be fun. Don't be inhibited by the "usual" way of doing things. Prove that you can clean your room in 10 minutes or less, or start at the bottom for once and work your way to the top. All of a sudden, for that brief period of time, cleaning your room ceases to be boring because it's different than you've ever done it!

USING YOUR CREATIVITY

At a seminar I asked everyone in the room to rate how creative they felt on a scale of 1 (least) to 10 (most). Then I asked them to rate how creative they would *like* to be. The average for the first question (actual feeling) was a 4. But the average for what they *wanted* to be was more than 8. Many people would like to be more creative, but don't know how. I offer them a definition to simplify their thinking: *Creativity is simply problem solving!*

Don't confuse being creative with being artistic. Artists create in one area, yet are not necessarily creative at all when it comes to problem solving in other areas. Nonartistic people can be very creative in those areas.

Every new idea that has entered your mind might be the solution to a problem. I used to sail paper plates and old records to see how far they would fly. But at some point someone thought, "I can improve on that," and used his creativity to invent the Frisbee! The Frisbee was a simple, inexpensive solution to the problem of boredom—and it has made millions of dollars!

If you are good at solving problems, you are a creative person. Begin thinking of yourself as creative. Become "impossible to bore," because creativity can evaporate boredom.

If you're bored, you can blame no one but yourself. No situation has to remain boring. You can simply create a new way to do the most boring thing on the face of the earth.

HOW WILL THIS APPLY WHEN I'M ON MY OWN?

Lots of adults spend most of their lives feeling bored. They feel like there's nothing new, invigorating, or fun.

Would it surprise you to learn that I have a lot of fun at work? When I'm at work I do things in somewhat uninhibited ways. I try to be spontaneous and creative. I enjoy my work. I enjoy coming up with ideas, concepts, principles, books, and solutions that have never, ever been tried before.

I am probably the hardest person on earth to bore. I would like to invite you to be the second hardest! What do you think?

KEY QUESTIONS

1. *When do you have the most fun?*
2. *When do you get bored most easily?*
3. *What boring things have you done this week that need to be creatively converted into fun activities?*

ACTION POINT

The next time you must perform some "boring" duty (such as doing the dishes or cleaning your room), think of a new and different way to do it. Start with one question: How can I use my creativity to overcome the boredom?

PRINCIPLE 34

"You can't win 'em all."—ROBERT L. BIEHL

"You can't have it all."—PHYLLIS RANEY

"You don't want it all."—BOBB BIEHL

One of the most common emotions in growing up is the sense of "failing again"—the feeling that no matter how hard you try, it isn't going to be good enough. My father frequently uses a phrase that helps take the sting out of some of life's "toe-stubbing experiences." He often says, "You can't win 'em all!"

YOU CAN'T WIN 'EM ALL
In life you will enjoy many victories and plenty of times when things go wonderfully well. But every person also has his or her share of stunning failures. You will go through times when, no matter how hard you try, you can't quite make something happen right. When you face such experiences, it's wise to remind yourself, "You can't win 'em all." (See Principle #14.)

YOU CAN'T HAVE IT ALL
Phyllis Raney is a friend who lives in Little Rock, Arkansas. One day she and I were discussing how many things were going right in another person's life, but how one particular thing had not worked out. Phyllis said, "Well, you can't have it all!"

Here again is practical wisdom. You can't do everything you want to do. You can't have all the dates you want. You can't win all the ballgames you play. You can't have all the cars you like.

That's why it's important to define your priorities and goals. For every goal you set, there are probably two or three other things you

116

can't do. If you go to a ballgame on Friday night, you won't be able to ride around in your car. You won't be able to study. You won't be able to go to church. There are many things you'll miss out on that night because you decided to go to a ballgame. You can't have it all.

YOU DON'T WANT IT ALL

A few years ago it became obvious to me that I really didn't want it all. If I had all the cars, all the clothes, and everything else I might imagine, think how cluttered my life would become!

Think how tired you would be if you went to all the games, studied all the subjects offered by your school, and attended every party. Think what it would be like to have every sweater you've ever wanted in your closet at one time. You really don't want it all.

HOW WILL THIS APPLY WHEN I'M ON MY OWN?

Adults must continually decide what they want and what they don't want. A lot of adults lead frustrated lives simply because they still believe you *can* win 'em all, you *can* have it all, and that they *do* want it all! As a result, they're burning themselves out. They stay tired, depressed, angry, and confused. Life would be so much simpler if they could come to grips with this principle as an adult.

Dr. James Dobson, the well-known Christian psychologist, tells the story of a little dog he used to have named Sigmund Freud. One day the Dobsons had a family dinner with spareribs as the main course. After dinner, they put all the bones in a trash bin and went away for a while.

Like most dogs, Sigmund Freud loved bones! When the Dobsons returned several hours later, they found the trash bin tipped over with bones lying all around. Off in a corner lay Sigmund Freud with his paws in four different directions, "sick as a dog" for having eaten so much.

Sigmund Freud had probably reasoned in his doggie mind, "Today is the day I get it all!" But it was actually the day he learned that he really didn't want it all!

Learning this lesson now will save you a tremendous amount of anxiety, frustration, and pressure as an adult.

KEY QUESTIONS

1. *What are the things you have "won at"—the things you've done right?*
2. *What things would you like to own if you possibly could?*
3. *What have you previously wanted, but later decided you really didn't want at all?*

ACTION POINT

Make a list in response to each of the three previous questions. Try to come up with 10 to 20 things on each list.

Don't be a "me, too" person. Learn to think and speak for yourself.

PRINCIPLE

35

Some people never seem to have an opinion on anything. They wait for someone else to speak or act, and then chime in with, "Me, too." They never think for themselves, stand out from the crowd, contribute to a conversation, or offer an opposing point of view.

THINK FOR YOURSELF
Don't go through life echoing the ideas of other people. Learn to think for yourself. One of the first things to do is memorize several questions to help bring you out of the "me, too" mode:

- Do I agree with what's being said?
- Do I believe what this person is saying, or am I being conned?
- Is this the way I would do it?
- If I had unlimited time, energy, or money, how would I do it differently?
- What is the ideal solution to this situation?
- Am I trying to "win," or just "get by"?

By asking yourself a few questions like these, you'll learn how to think for yourself. You'll develop confidence to form your own opinions and reach your own conclusions.

SPEAK FOR YOURSELF
Before you can learn to speak for yourself, you must learn to think for yourself. Once your thoughts are clear, it's much easier to speak.

119

You may want to preface your thoughts with an introductory phrase such as, "Is it possible that . . . ," "I think another way to do it might be . . . ," "Would it help if we . . . ," or something similar.

You don't need to express yourself with an arrogant, "pushy" style. You want develop confidence, not become obnoxious. As you begin to think and speak for yourself, you will contribute much more to life than if you always fall back on the comfortable, secure phrase, "Me, too."

KEY QUESTIONS

1.*Do you find it difficult to think for yourself?*
2.*Do you find it difficult to speak for yourself?*
3.*How do you overcome the difficulties of thinking and speaking for yourself?*

ACTION POINT

Make a list of things you want to be able to think independently about, rather than being swayed by popular opinion (drug use, premarital sex, social drinking, abortion, etc.). First, *think* these issues through to reach your own independent conclusions, and then be prepared to *speak* for yourself as well.

Good manners should be part of both masculine and feminine development.

PRINCIPLE

36

"Etiquette is for sissies!"
"Don't bother trying to teach me manners, I'm a tomboy."
"My manners are terrible, but who cares? I sure don't!"

When we're little kids, few of us care too much about good manners. Who needs them? To a young boy, manners seem sissyish. To a young girl who is a tomboy, manners seem too feminine and restricting. Our general attitude begins as, "I ain't got no manners and I don't want none!"

GOOD MANNERS KNOW NO GENDER
Both men and women need a good grasp of etiquette—table manners, social manners, and professional manners. We need to know how to relate to people in a predictable way. It should be automatic to say "thank you" after receiving something and "please" when asking for something. We need to be gracious, kind, loving, and considerate. Good manners are never out of place.

It can be embarrassing to be at a major social event and not know which fork to use, how to address a person properly, how to make gracious introductions, or how to behave in general. An ignorance of good manners can quickly damage your reputation. This is why it is important to begin watching parents and other adults while you can. You may even want to consider taking a class that teaches basic etiquette.

Young kids can get by with an ignorance of proper conduct. But as adults, both men and women without manners can be labeled by others as obnoxious.

In short, good manners aren't just for sissies. They shouldn't be optional for tomboys. Rather, they should be important to each person. Begin now to develop manners you won't be ashamed of.

KEY QUESTIONS

1. *On a scale of one to ten, how would you rate your manners?*
2. *What adult man do you know with the best manners? What adult woman?*
3. *How can you improve in this area?*

ACTION POINT

Identify one person who would probably be the best teacher for you in the area of developing outstanding manners. Ask that person if he or she will teach you how to improve in this area. You will be thankful that you did for the rest of your life.

Master the art of being positive. No one enjoys being with negative complainers!

Do you know anyone who is negative about *everything*—never happy or optimistic? That attitude tends to rub off quickly, but life is too short to spend all your time looking at the dark side of things. Don't get in the habit of looking at the negative side of life.

Negative comments lead to a negative attitude. A negative attitude leads to negative comments. Pretty soon you're in a whirlpool dragging you to the depths of despair. If you should ever find yourself developing this negative cycle, discipline yourself to start thinking in positive terms as quickly as you possibly can.

THE ART OF BEING POSITIVE

People may accuse you of being unrealistic if you choose to look on the positive side rather than the negative. But it's no more unrealistic than being negative all the time. It's simply a choice.

Scripture tells us, "Whatever is true, whatever is noble, whatever is right, whatever is pure, whatever is lovely, whatever is admirable—if anything is excellent or praiseworthy—think about such things" (Philippians 4:8, NIV). The Bible recommends that we think, reflect, and meditate on positive things.

But please look closely at this Scripture as you try to develop a positive attitude. Don't be misled. Another similar-sounding philosophy is to have a "positive mental attitude" (PMA)—an approach to life which says, "I can do everything I set out to do." The focus is put on the individual instead of God. It's not wrong to have positive confidence about the future, but it is essential to recognize that God is the source of our confidence. There is danger in being too confident in our own ability and not relying on God.

NO ONE LIKES A WHINER

How many negative complainers do you enjoy being with? How many people like to be with *you* when you complain and bellyache about everything that happens?

If you want to lose friends fast, start complaining about everything they do. They will soon begin to avoid you. When you feel negative, it's a good idea to get it out of your system so you can be positive as quickly as possible.

Which would you rather have, your friends or your negative attitude? The choice is yours.

KEY QUESTIONS

1. *Do people see you as positive or negative?*
2. *What are the top three things you like about each of your friends and family members?*
3. *What are three positive things about your school, church, youth group, etc.?*

ACTION POINT

Make a list of the top three positive things about every person, situation, and organization you're involved with. It is a very healthy, positive thing to do.

Also ask your parents and close friends to be honest with how they see you—as positive or negative. They may have a different perspective than you do.

A mistake is only a failure . . . if you don't learn from it.

ROLAND NIEDNAGEL

Every person alive has felt the sting of failure. After trying hard and missing the mark completely, we may feel like just giving up. But when you feel like this, remember that a mistake is only a failure if you don't learn from it.

MISTAKES AND FAILURES

No one wants to fail. People don't go around looking for ways to mess up. If someone drops a pass in the last seconds of the game, says the wrong thing at a party, or misses a deadline, it doesn't mean he or she is a failure. The person simply made a mistake.

We *all* make mistakes. Everyone deserves the freedom to be less than perfect without facing rejection. Yet many people have an intense fear of failure—not only teenagers, but adults as well. Some people grow up feeling if they aren't perfect, others won't love them. But anyone who would reject you because of a mistake doesn't really love you. All of the people who really, truly love you will understand that a mistake is a mistake, and will let you make a few (actually, a lot) in the process of growing up.

LEARNING FROM FAILURE

Some failures are simply part of a learning process—learning to water-ski, for example. In the beginning you fall down over and over . . . but you try again and again. Each time you fall, you try to learn what to do differently next time to get it right.

Anytime you make a mistake, stop and ask yourself, "What have I learned from this?" That question helps you turn mistakes into valuable learning experiences.

HOW WILL THIS APPLY WHEN I'M ON MY OWN?
Failure is certainly not limited to the teenage years! You're going to be imperfect for the rest of your life. You'll still occasionally make mistakes, say the wrong things, make bad choices, and so forth!

In fact, adults tend to make mistakes with bigger financial or life-changing consequences. Yet wise adults never stop learning from their mistakes, correcting them, and moving on.

When you get a chance, watch some babies learning to walk. They can't seem to master the ability of putting one foot in front of the other and staying upright without falling flat on their diaper-cushioned rumps! But what do they do? They get up and try again!

What if babies thought people would reject them if they fell down? They wouldn't want to risk trying again. But when they sense that the adult world enjoys seeing them try to walk and is cheering them on, they keep trying till they get it right.

Sometimes adults get frustrated with how long it takes a teenager to learn from a mistake. But we also realize it's an important part of learning how to handle the pressures of adulthood.

I'll never forget when my son was beginning to climb trees, at about age 4. The immediate panic of parents is, "Oh, he'll fall and break an arm or a leg." But my wife and I decided to let him give it his best shot. We knew it was part of his growing-up process. He would soon learn he can't step into thin air and still stay in a tree!

Fortunately, without breaking any bones, my son did develop the ability to climb trees—and later to do just about anything else he cared to. Today he has a confidence at heights he wouldn't have if his mom and dad had held a safety net under every tree he ever tried to climb.

We adults are in the process of letting you grow up, one mistake at a time, realizing you will learn from each one just as we did. That's why we can tell you with complete confidence, "You're gonna make it!"

126

KEY QUESTIONS

1. *What are some mistakes you've made in life?*
2. *What have you learned from them?*
3. *How do you know your parents still love you, even though you've made mistakes here and there?*

ACTION POINT

Get a blank sheet of paper and draw a line to divide it into two columns. Put "FAILURES" at the top of the left column. Down the left side of the paper, list all the failures you've had during the past year. Next, mark out the word "FAILURES" and replace it with the word "MISTAKES." On the right side of your paper write out what you learned from each of those mistakes. From now on, don't think of your shortcomings as failures ever again. Rather, count them as mistakes you have learned from!

PRINCIPLE 39

"Life without goals is like a race without a finish line."

ED TRENNER

Sometimes your future can get pretty blurry. It becomes difficult to figure out what your next steps should be. It feels like you're running in a dense fog and could tumble off a cliff or smash into a brick wall. As a result, you tend to slow down and just creep along at a snail's pace. This is a very common experience if you don't have clear goals.

DEFINING GOALS
The minute I mention the word *goals*, a lot of people become tense or nervous because they have learned to equate goals with failure. But goals are simple to create and use. I define a goal as "A realistic, measurable target in the future."

A goal may be, "I want to go to the ballgame on Friday." Such a statement is realistic and measurable. On Saturday morning, you know whether you reached your goal or not. Other goals are more complex, such as landing a manned space shuttle on Mars by the year 2050. But just like planning to attend the game, this is a realistic and measurable goal.

USING GOALS
We can use our goals to determine if we are successful or not. If you have clear, realistic, measurable goals, you feel like you've succeeded if you reach them. This does not mean you are a failure in life if you don't reach all your goals. It simply means you failed to reach those

particular goals on time. If you reach even 50 percent of the goals you set, you're in great shape! Having goals gives you a track to run on in the race of life!

SETTING GOALS

Are you a person who tends to equate goals with failure? Have you set goals in the past and ended up feeling overwhelmed, frustrated, and discouraged because you didn't reach them? There are three primary reasons people establish goals that are "setups for failure."

(1) *Setting goals when on an emotional high.* Don't set goals when you're very enthused and then try to carry them out when you're not. (This happens a lot in group goal setting.) It is much better to wait until you are at a more balanced emotional level to set goals.

(2) *Setting goals where you have no track record.* If you've never done something before, don't set goals in that area until you've had an opportunity to experiment. (Or as they say on dairy farms, "Don't brag about how many gallons of milk you can get out of a cow until you've milked her once.")

(3) *Setting high goals to "impress the boss."* People who set unrealistically high goals may impress their managers—until the boss realizes they're simply going to fail. When this happens, the very thing they wanted to do (impress the boss) turns out to have the exact opposite result. They end up disappointing the boss. It is far better to set realistic goals and then try to exceed them!

It may take months or years to become good at setting clear, measurable, realistic goals . . . and hitting a high percentage of them. But over your lifetime, make this a constant effort. There are few things in life more important than setting goals and then "crossing the finish line!"

HOW WILL THIS APPLY WHEN I'M ON MY OWN?

People need goals to motivate them for the future, to communicate basic directions to other people, and to measure success. When people don't have goals, they end up running just as hard, but going in circles. Learn to avoid the dangerous condition of running hard in a dense fog, and maybe going over a cliff. Learn to set goals!

KEY QUESTIONS

1. *What one specific goal would you like to set for the next 30 days?*
2. *If you could only do three things this year, what would you do? (Make sure these things are realistic, measurable, and time dated.)*
3. *If you could only do one measurable, realistic thing between now and the time you die, what one thing would you most want to accomplish?*

ACTION POINT

List the three most important things you need to accomplish during the next seven days. (Remember: keep them realistic and measurable.) Determine the top three things for the next 30 days . . . then 90 days . . . then the next year.

Don't become overly concerned if you don't reach every single goal you set. Just keep working and reevaluating. Allow your goals to give you a clear focus for the future!

**Listen to God.
Listen to yourself.
Listen to trusted family
and friends.
And ignore the crowd.**

Whenever you find yourself becoming too concerned about what other people think about you, think about the ridiculous cheers some crowds begin to chant at a desperate person on a ten-story ledge: "Jump! Jump! Jump!" The crowd does not have your best interests at heart.

You may be aware of people at school who would be happy to have you start doing drugs. Perhaps they would make money from it. It might convince them that if you do it, they must not be so bad off. Maybe they just want to see you get high and make a fool of yourself. Other people want to cheat on exams and encourage everyone else to join in their dishonesty. But it's important to do what's right in your own eyes, rather than simply follow the crowd!

LISTEN TO GOD
As you will discover in Principle #87, the Bible is the only authoritative source of complete truth. The more you read the Bible, the more you learn about God, His view of your situation, and His values. Listen first of all to the truth of the Bible instead of automatically going along with the crowd.

LISTEN TO YOURSELF
You have an inner voice that tells you right from wrong most of the time. You know when you're supposed to do (or not do) something. Listen to yourself far more than you listen to the crowd.

LISTEN TO TRUSTED FAMILY AND FRIENDS

Not every acquaintance you have is a true friend. Occasionally there may even be a family member who is not genuinely concerned about your welfare. But for the most part, you have the ability to decide whom you can trust among your family members and friends. You know who are the wisest and most balanced. Learn to listen to these people even when they don't push their advice on you. I've often said, "The crowd can scream something at me, and I will still hear the whisper of a trusted family member or friend."

IGNORE THE CROWD

One of the dramatic realizations a person comes to at about age 20 is that his or her high school crowd tends to drift apart. Some go to college. Some go to the military. Some go to trade school. Some go to work. The influential crowd that used to seem so important is scattered to the four corners of the earth. In one sense, you are left with yourself, God, and the mirror. Perhaps your closest friends keep in touch. But over time you realize "the crowd" really doesn't have much interest in your long-term well-being.

On the other hand, you know that God and your trusted family and friends will continue to try to help you make decisions that will be best for you for the rest of your life.

HOW WILL THIS APPLY WHEN I'M ON MY OWN?

Even adults tend to develop a "crowd we're trying to please." And they can suffer the consequences of it just like a young person can. This principle is just as valuable in adulthood as it is at any other time. It is extremely helpful advice to rely on throughout your lifetime.

KEY QUESTIONS

1. *What decision are you trying to make right now? What do you feel God has to say about this decision in the Bible?*

2. *What do you feel about this decision personally? Do you feel in your heart of hearts and think in your private thoughts that it's right . . . or wrong?*

132

3. *Who are the two or three family members and close friends you trust most? What is their thinking on the decision you're trying to make?*

ACTION POINT
As you try to make the critical decision you're considering at this moment, listen to God, listen to yourself, listen to trusted family and friends . . . and ignore the crowd!

PRINCIPLE

41

To feel organized, have a place for everything, and everything in its place.

How many times have you felt totally disorganized, when everything was a mess? After you get to that point, trying to get organized again seems like an impossible task. That is not an uncommon feeling for teenagers (or adults) to have. But how do we go about regaining that feeling of being organized?

HOW TO FEEL ORGANIZED

I use the word "feel" because it best describes organization. Some people feel organized when a group of ten judges would say they're not organized at all. Some people feel disorganized when others would say they are very organized. So, how does a person get the feeling of being organized?

Some people never seem to have a specific place for anything—no place in the closet for shoes, no place in the kitchen for the silverware, no place in the locker for books. With no place for everything, they end up stacking, piling, or throwing things all over. That leaves them feeling very disorganized.

If you have a place for your things, you feel more organized, even when those things aren't in their places. Yet when those things *are* in their places, so much the better.

You can attend all the seminars, listen to all the experts, and read all the books, but you won't find a method of organization any better than what most of our grandmothers have told us: "Have a place for everything and everything in its place!"

HOW WILL THIS APPLY WHEN I'M ON MY OWN?

As a teenager you're in the process of forming habits you'll carry into adulthood. The more organized you are about things today, the greater your head start for your adult years.

In college, a friend of mine "fell in love" with a beautiful girl from my hometown. My friend started dating the girl and eventually took her to meet his parents, 300 miles away. While she was there, her room looked like a hurricane had hit it! Items from her suitcase were spread everywhere. My friend's mother told him privately, "Go see if that's the way you'd like your house to look when you're married. The habits she has now will follow her into adulthood."

My friend was a particularly tidy person. His car was always washed, waxed, and vacuumed. His room was always extremely neat. His desk was always meticulously organized. I remember him saying to me, "I really like that girl and think I could be happily married to her, but I couldn't stand her messy habits."

This example is not meant to infer that if you don't pick up your clothes, you'll never get married! The simple point is, the organization habits we form in junior high, high school, and college will last us for a lifetime.

KEY QUESTIONS

1. *What are the areas you are responsible for keeping organized?*
2. *Do you have a place for everything you are responsible for?*
3. *How can you keep everything in its place?*

ACTION POINT

Identify your most cluttered area. It could be your locker, your room, or your car. Then simply go clean it up. Put everything in its rightful place and experience the feeling of being personally organized.

PRINCIPLE 42

Success is the feeling you get when you reach your goals!

People today seem to be endlessly seeking success! We want to be more successful in sports, school, careers, and social standing. And we don't just want to *be* successful; we also want to *look* successful.

DEFINING SUCCESS
What is success? I spend a lot of time working with presidents of companies, trying to help them understand and define success. These are some of the things I've discovered:

- *There seems to be no common definition of success that everyone accepts and understands.*
- *People tend to set a definition that's meaningful to them, and then try to make others adopt their standards.* For example, one person may define success as having a big house. But that wouldn't indicate success to you if you didn't even want a big house.
- *After achieving a stated measure of success, sometimes people change the definition!* A friend may say success is making the basketball team. So you make the basketball team and hope he'll think you've succeeded. But then he says, "Truly successful people are also in the Honor Society."

After dealing with many presidents and senior pastors over the years, I've concluded that success is the feeling you get when you reach your goals! Success is a *feeling*, not a tangible reality or a lifetime accomplishment. That's why "success" is so difficult to hang on to. When you reach your goals and feel successful, you usually set new, higher goals to reach. Feelings of success frequently come and go!

THE IMPORTANCE OF GOALS

Many people set foggy, unmeasurable goals like, "This year I will do the very best I can." At the end of the year, there is no way for them to evaluate whether or not they've done as well as they could.

Goals are also relative. You shouldn't try to compare your goals to someone else's. The success you expect should be based on your goals alone. For example, a person who sets a goal of making $90,000 a year and makes $100,000 should feel successful. In fact, that person is likely to feel more successful than someone who sets a goal to make $1,000,000 and only makes $900,000. If your goals are realistic and measurable, you feel successful when you reach them.

The average person who sets goals to have a house, a car, and enough money to pay the bills feels pretty successful when he or she meets those goals. But if that person adopts someone else's definition of success, he may spend his life chasing bigger cars, bigger houses, and more money—and never feeling successful.

To feel successful in life, decide what goals you really want to reach and go after them. When you achieve them, you'll have a feeling of success regardless of what other people have or have not done. The sooner you realize it's your definition of success that's important, not someone else's, the sooner you will have mastered the idea of success.

KEY QUESTIONS

1. *Why haven't you felt successful in the past?*
2. *What goals would you like to set?*
3. *As you've reached goals in the past, have you had a feeling of success?*

ACTION POINT

Make a list of your goals for the next 30 to 90 days. As you reach each one, check it off and see if you don't have a rewarding feeling of success.

PHYSICAL

PRINCIPLES

No body is perfect . . . accept yours!

PRINCIPLE

43

Have you ever stood in front of a mirror naked and wondered to yourself, "How did I get stuck with this body?" Nose too long. Lips too large. Ears sticking out too far. Teeth too crooked. Hands too small. Legs too short. Hips too wide. The list could go on and on!

Whenever you get caught in the "hyper-analyze my body" trap, there are three reminders to help you regain your perspective and begin to let you like yourself again. They are:

    (1) If you compare, be fair!

    (2) Make the best of what you do have—highlight and camouflage.

    (3) Be thankful for what you have!

IF YOU COMPARE, BE FAIR!

The best position to take in life is to compare yourself to no one. Simply accept yourself as you are. Understand that God made you. You are acceptable to Him. He loves you. Seek to maximize who you are. Don't try so hard to become more like someone else and less like yourself.

I know it is far easier to give this advice than it is to actually do it. But if you must compare, be fair to yourself. There will always be someone who is skinnier or fatter, more or less muscular, taller or shorter than you.

Never compare yourself with those who have been singled out for their attractiveness. If you do, you will probably come out

141

feeling like a loser. If you start trying to compete with magazine cover girls or muscle magazine models, you can always find a way to make yourself feel like an "ugly ducking." Those people have a lot of money and time invested solely into looking good. It is unrealistic for you to expect to look that way.

Never compare yourself with a magazine picture. The model in that picture may have a terrible personality, dietary problems, ugly feet, or any number of other problems that you don't see. Just make your life as good as it can be and don't waste a lot of time wishing you looked like someone else. Be fair to yourself.

MAKE THE BEST OF WHAT YOU DO HAVE

My daughter Kimberly lives in Hollywood, California. She has worked at major talent agencies and knows many professional models, actors, and actresses. She says that she does not know of a single one who is not self-conscious about some part of his or her body. They all go to great lengths to keep such characteristics from being featured.

Every person is a combination of attractive features and not-so-attractive features. The most attractive of people are self-conscious about certain parts of their bodies. So if even world-class models and famous television/movie actors and actresses try to downplay their undesired features, so can you.

Learn to highlight, feature, and compliment your good points. Hide or camouflage your less-attractive features. Seek help from makeup clerks, clothing sales personnel, and friends. Everyone has a number of helpful suggestions they will probably share with you.

BE THANKFUL FOR WHAT YOU HAVE!

If you focus on what you don't have, you will never be content. Rather, be thankful for what you do have: your health, the fact that you can breathe without pain, your ability to walk, talk, see, hear, and so forth. As you know, many people do not have these privileges.

Tap into the truth that real friends and lifelong mates will be attracted to your character far more than your hair color, and to your personality more than a perfect profile.

Remember this old Russian proverb:

> When you meet a man, you judge him by his clothes.
> When you leave a man, you judge him by his heart.

KEY QUESTIONS

1. *What part of your body do you most want to feature?*
2. *What part of your body do you most want to camouflage?*
3. *Who do you admire—and trust—to help you learn how to make the most of what you have?*

ACTION POINT

Make a list of all the things you like about your body—especially the points you want to feature. Also list all of the things for which you are thankful.

PRINCIPLE

44

Form healthy habits while you are young!

You have already formed many habits in life. Some you want to keep. Some you wish you could break. But by now you are a creature of habit.

In the next ten years you will form perhaps another hundred lifelong habits. Why not decide today to form some healthy habits which will remain with you for a lifetime?

Habits help you "internalize" your discipline. This simply means that you develop certain habit patterns of eating, drinking, thinking, etc. regardless of who is or is not around. Here is the beginning of a list of habits to consider developing. You can add to the suggestions on this list as well as adding new categories.

EATING
I will develop a lifelong habit of:
> Avoiding excessive fried foods, fats, salt, and sugar
> Regulating the amount of junk food I eat
> Eating a balanced diet
> Not overeating.

DRINKING
I will develop a lifelong habit of:
> Avoiding alcohol
> Drinking lots of water and natural fruit juices
> Restricting the amount of caffeine in my drinks.

THINKING

I will develop a lifelong habit of:

Thinking positively, not negatively

Focusing on pure thoughts, not evil ones

Concentrating on the future, not the failures of the past

Thinking more about solutions than problems.

After you develop a habit, it's hard to get rid of it. So why not have habits that will benefit you rather than harm you? Whether it is a matter of driving, sleeping, relating to others, or whatever, form healthy habits today . . . while you are young. When you are older, you won't be sorry.

KEY QUESTIONS

1. *What eating habits should you start forming today?*
2. *What drinking habits should you start forming today?*
3. *What thinking (or other) habits should you start forming today?*

ACTION POINT

Ask three adults you respect a great deal what eating, drinking, and thinking habits they wish they had formed when they were your age.

PRINCIPLE

45

Take a shower a day . . . or friends (and dates) stay away!

Probably the most common piece of advice given by mothers to children worldwide is: "Wear clean underwear in case you have an accident and need to see a doctor!"

You may not be surprised that I would suggest that number two should be, "Take a shower a day . . . or friends (and dates) stay away!"

Remember this for the rest of your life, no matter where you go or what you do: *Clean and fresh is always far more attractive than dirty and smelly!*

WORTH THE EFFORT

This principle is an obvious one, yet you have probably known people who seemed unaware of it. Perhaps one of the most depressing experiences you can have is to be around someone who is a wonderful person, lots of fun, a person you would like to spend time with—yet whose body odor always keeps other people at a distance.

Sometimes it takes work to stay clean and fresh. When we get lazy, we run the risk of losing friends or dates. So always use deodorant. Brush your teeth regularly. Use breath fresheners. Change your socks and tennis shoes frequently. In short, smell clean and fresh!

If you ever wonder if you might have a problem with offensive odors, don't be afraid to ask a friend! (More than likely, others are looking for the right opportunity to tell you.) And keep in mind that being clean and fresh also applies to your room, your car, your bathroom, your kitchen area, and everywhere else you go. It's hard to be too clean or too fresh, so keep looking for ways to improve.

There are very few things in life which will cost you more friends and dates than offensive odors or lack of personal hygiene.

KEY QUESTIONS
1.*How do you feel about a friend with strong body odor?*
2.*How do you feel about a friend with bad breath?*
3.*How do you feel about a friend with a dirty car, bedroom, bathroom, etc.?*

ACTION POINT
Ask your mother, father, or a close friend to tell you the absolute truth about any hygiene problems you may have and not be aware of. Then take an inventory of your bathroom and see if you are in need of any items such as soap, mouthwash, deodorant, breath mints, etc. Make a run to the store and stock up on anything you need.

Find a sport that fits you!

Some people are naturals when it comes to sports. They seem to excel at everything they try to do. I wasn't one of those people. I felt that because I didn't like the most popular sports at school, that sports were out for me. If only my coaches in junior and senior high school had told me that there are hundreds of sports, my whole life may well have taken a very different turn. If you are like me and think you aren't cut out for sports, simply try to find one that fits you.

In our high school the popular sports (football, basketball, and baseball) all required people who were much faster, taller, or heavier than I was. As a result, I played only a little and starred at nothing. I hope that today a wise coach would advise a person like me to take up golf, swimming, wrestling, or a wide variety of other sports which do not require exceptional speed or size.

A recent television special on the Olympics showed that there are over 200 special shoes designed for the many varieties of athletic events. It follows that you must have a large selection of sports to participate in. Certainly you can find one that fits your special combination of brain and brawn. Ask a coach you trust to help you identify your special abilities and match those to a sport which is a good fit for you.

WHY FIND A SPORT AT ALL?

People enjoy sports for different reasons. Some enjoy the competition, some the companionship, some the exercise, and some just for the break in their regular routine. Later in life a lot of business is likely to be conducted on the golf course, tennis court, or in some other athletic setting.

So look for a new sport that may appeal to you. Try new and different things: swimming, horseback riding, bowling, jogging, bicycling, racquetball, Frisbee throwing, or whatever you think you would enjoy doing. It doesn't have to involve a big crowd or be competitive at all.

It is important to know, however, that not everyone has the same energy level, interest, or need to be involved in athletics. If you are not "into sports," don't force yourself to be miserable just because you think you need to be more of an athlete. Relax and watch other people play, or simply ignore sports altogether. But with a little searching, most people will find something they truly enjoy doing and will get better at it with practice.

KEY QUESTIONS

1. *What individual or team sport would best fit you?*

2. *How interested are you in becoming really good in this sport?*

3. *Who could help you reach your full potential in this sport if it is not popular among your friends?*

ACTION POINT

Ask a trusted coach to help you choose a sport that is best for you—both now, and ideally when you are 60, 70, or 80 years old as well.

PRINCIPLE

47

Sports are a vital element of our lives, but should never become the main goal of life.

Have you ever known a "sports nut"? Sports nuts eat, sleep, and dream sports! They hardly know how to have a conversation on any topic other than sports. Sports is their world. Sports is their identity. Sports is their focus. Sports is their life!

SPORTS IS A MEANS, NOT AN END!

Sports are good because they help us build healthy bodies and learn team play, sportsmanship, and discipline. Sports add to our self-esteem (when we play well). And they provide a great deal of entertainment for spectators as well as participants.

However, sports can also become the basis of our identities, or our primary hope of a college education or a living beyond college in pro sports. When this happens, we are in great danger of letting sports become an end rather than a means. The harm it can do to our life-styles is greater than the potential benefit of a healthier body or the development of teamwork.

So at this point I offer a warning: If your self-concept is based on being able to say, "I am a jock," beware! I have seen many "jocks" get injured and lose all sense of self-confidence. Their sense of value rested on their ability to hit a ball or set a school record. When they were injured, their lives seemed to "come to an end."

Build your life on God, relationships, academic ability, character, and other truly important foundations. Your athletic ability can add to your other strengths, but it can never replace them.

150

SPORTS AND SPOUSES

One of the important discussions for you to have with a person you are dating seriously, especially if you are considering the possibility of marriage, is your level of involvement with athletic interests. Recently I had a conversation with a divorced man who said, "Shortly after we were married we realized we had very little in common. . . . My life was sports. . . . She had no interest of any kind in sports at any level."

This is not to say that you must have identical interests. But before you say "I do," you may want to ask your future mate a few basic questions. Would he or she prefer going to a concert or to a football game? Would he or she rather watch a game or play in it? Does he or she prefer to be outdoors or indoors? And so forth.

After you talk through some of these basic questions, you will both have a much better understanding of how the other person thinks and feels about sporting events. And athletic events will tend to bring you closer together rather than tear you apart.

KEY QUESTIONS

1. *How important are sports to you?*
2. *What part would you prefer that sports play in your dating/marriage?*
3. *Would you rather play sports or watch them?*

ACTION POINT

If you see yourself as a "jock," talk with a trusted adviser about broadening your self-image beyond this one concept.

If you are not a "jock," define what percentage of your life you want to be devoted to athletics (participating or watching) over a lifetime.

Flee from sexual immorality.

(I Corinthians 6:18a, NIV)

48

Premarital sexual intercourse is one activity which for many has provided minutes of forbidden pleasure and resulted in years of pain—pregnancy, abortion, sexually transmitted diseases, guilt, and more. In the Bible, we are warned: "Flee from sexual immorality. All other sins a man commits are outside his body, but he who sins sexually sins against his own body. Do you not know that your body is a temple of the Holy Spirit, who is in you, whom you have received from God? You are not your own; you were bought at a price. Therefore honor God with your body" (I Corinthians 6:18-20, NIV).

SEX: THEN AND NOW

In the past few decades, society's attitudes toward sexual immorality have changed drastically. Until the 1960s, premarital sex was frowned upon by the "good girls" of most schools. Those couples who had premarital sex were looked down on. Girls were expected to say, "No" and boys were expected to try to get them to say, "Yes." The main deterrent for a dating couple was fear of being exposed via an unwanted pregnancy.

If the girl became pregnant, the socially responsible thing for the couple to do was to get married and hope the child never learned that Mom was pregnant before marriage and that he or she was an unwanted child. The option of abortion was available for the lower class only through back-alley butchers, or for the extremely wealthy through unethical doctors who performed them illegally. The possibility of sexually transmitted diseases was very slight. The threat of AIDS was nonexistent.

But social values changed very rapidly from 1960 until 1981. "Free Love" was the theme of the hippies in San Francisco, and this appealing theme spread across the country and around the world. By the late 70s, virgins were frequently the ones who seemed "out of it." Girls were no longer expected to say no. If a pregnancy occurred, abortion clinics were readily available to provide seemingly simple, affordable, available procedures with no lingering problems. Sex was "out in the open." Biblical values were considered prudish and were laughed at by nonbelievers (and, sad to say, some believers). Sexually transmitted diseases were still rare and as yet no threat of AIDS was known.

In 1981 the first case of AIDS was reported. Soon the number of cases reported began to double with each passing year. By the late 1980s AIDS had spread beyond the homosexual community into mainstream America. Experts now tell us the disease will cost billions of dollars and that they expect more than 100 million deaths worldwide by the year 2000. Sexually transmitted diseases, once thought to be found only among prostitutes, are now experienced by millions—some resulting in death.

TRUST YOUR STEERING MORE THAN YOUR BRAKES

Remember that if you choose to have sex with a person, you put yourself at risk from everyone that person has ever had sex with in the past. That's why today, as never before in history, I Corinthians 6:18-20 is wise counsel for any person about to be on his or her own. It is far better to flee from sexual immorality and honor God with your body than to take a risk that could destroy your relationship with Him, your reputation, your health, or even your life.

Even with all of this frightening information about the severe cost of premarital sex, the temptation remains strong. Therefore, it is important to "steer clear" of situations where you are likely to be tempted sexually. Otherwise, you must depend heavily on your "brakes" when you find yourself in a sexual situation. You shouldn't put much trust in your "just say no" brakes during a passionate

153

moment. It is far safer to avoid the situation altogether.

The biblical advice provided by this principle is not to sidestep temptation at the last possible moment. Rather, we are to flee from sexual immorality. This is very wise advice indeed.

KEY QUESTIONS

1. *How important is it to you to be a virgin when you marry?*
2. *What steps do you plan to take to flee from immorality in this age of sexual activity and AIDS?*
3. *If you are not a virgin, how do you plan to handle sexual situations in the future? (You should decide now, and not in the heat of a passionate moment.)*

ACTION POINT

Talk to your parents or a trusted friend about any questions you have about sex. You might first want to prepare a written list of questions to avoid embarrassment during the conversation.

When you see a person with a handicap, focus on the person more than the handicap!

PRINCIPLE

49

Imagine that one of your close friends is in an accident and left handicapped in some way. Would that person cease to be your friend? No, of course not. He or she would continue to be a person who feels, thinks, and needs love.

But what about a person with a handicap whom you meet for the first time? Sometimes people have a lot of trouble trying to initiate any kind of communication with handicapped people. What do you do around them? What do you say to them?

The suggestions on pages 156 and 157 are provided by Joni and Friends in Agoura, California. (Joni Eareckson Tada became a quadriplegic after a diving accident as a teenager.) Read through this list, think of people with whom you might be able to implement some of the suggestions, and answer the following questions.

KEY QUESTIONS
1. *What would you want done for you if you had a handicap?*
2. *What one thing could you do to help a person with a handicap?*
3. *What would be your first step in getting started?*

ACTION POINT
Think seriously for a few minutes what role you could play in helping a person with a handicap. Get a specific person in mind and list the first steps you might take toward actually helping him or her.

24 WAYS TO HELP A DISABLED FRIEND

Non-disabled people often say, "I'd like to be helpful to handi-capped people, but I don't really know what to do." Here are a few suggestions for starters that may spark some better ideas of your own.

(1) Get acquainted with at least one handicapped person in your church. Go beyond the "Good morning. . . . How are you? . . . I'm fine, thanks. . . . Have a nice day" stage and really get to know him or her.

(2) If you know a blind person, offer to come to his or her home on a regular basis and read the print mail.

(3) Survey your church to determine how accessible it is for the mobility impaired—sanctuary, restrooms, fellowship hall, pastor's office, and any other rooms frequently used for meetings. Ask the advice of any disabled person in the congregation when making such a survey.

(4) Spearhead a committee to raise funds for an elevator or a ramp if your church needs one.

(5) If there is a curb between the parking lot and the church, ramp it or build a curb cut.

(6) Make an effort to include handicapped people in church gatherings such as fellowship suppers, women's circle meetings, Bible study and prayer meetings, and socials. Isolation is a health hazard!

(7) Install amplifying devices at various places throughout the church for the hearing impaired.

(8) Ask someone who is hearing impaired if the lighting is sufficient in the church. Those who read lips find it hard to do so when the lighting is poor.

(9) Be aware of families with disabled children. It may be difficult for the parents to find experienced baby-sitters, but they, too, need an evening out now and then. Offer your services.

(10) Offer transportation to a handicapped person on a regular basis.

(11) Purchase large-print hymnbooks or Bibles for those who need them at your church.

(12) Learn to write braille, and braille the hymns or the sermon text for blind members each week.

(13) Learn some basic sign language. It's a loving gesture for a deaf person.

(14) Free a person in a wheelchair from being housebound by building a ramp into his or her home.

(15) Remind yourself that a handicap is a condition, not a disease. Sit next to a blind, deaf, or cerebral-palsied person. Share in the meeting, and get acquainted afterward.

(16) Keep your eyes and ears open for jobs that might be done by a disabled person at your place of employment. Encourage the hiring of a handicapped employee.

(17) Don't park your car in spaces designated for the disabled.

(18) If you want to help a blind person cross a street or move to another part of the building, ask if he would like assistance. Let him take your arm and lead him. Do not grab his arm and propel him ahead of you.

(19) Tell someone about the Christian League for the Handicapped.

(20) Suggest that your organization take on a love project . . . rake lawns, do minor repair jobs, wash windows, etc., for disabled homeowners in your church or neighborhood.

(21) Remember that handicapped church members often have talents and skills which are needed. Ask them to help with phoning chores, serving on committees, singing, teaching Sunday school, or whatever is appropriate to their abilities.

(22) If you think assistance might be needed, do not hesitate to ask disabled persons how you might help. They can tell you the easiest and safest way.

(23) Hold the door for a person in a wheelchair or on crutches in a shopping center, at church, or wherever. It's common courtesy, but often overlooked.

(24) Just be friendly. "So then, while we have opportunity, let us do good to all men, and especially to those who are of the household of faith" (Galatians 6:10, NASB).

PRINCIPLE 50

"Fatigue makes cowards of us all."

COACH VINCE LOMBARDI

Vince Lombardi, coach of the two-time Superbowl Champion Green Bay Packers in the 60s, insisted that his players get to bed early before each game. He said, "Fatigue makes cowards of us all." He knew that a tired player in the fourth quarter can miss that one critical tackle that loses the game. He won't be able to spring to his feet like he normally could or pursue an opponent like he should.

I have thought about Coach Lombardi's quote for a number of years, and I'd like to add: "Fatigue also makes us self-centered and negative." When we're overly tired, we begin questioning ourselves and our abilities. We become negative, complaining, consumed with thinking about ourselves, and generally irritable.

FATIGUE

Fatigue is a point beyond feeling a little tired. Fatigue doesn't occur in one day. But after several nights without much sleep, while working or playing hard all day, we can get to where even when we wake up in the morning we are still tired. That's fatigue.

There are two kinds of energy: natural energy and forced energy. Natural energy is when you wake up in the morning feeling great. You feel like playing sports, going to school, or going to work. Forced energy is when you have to force yourself to get out of bed, go to school, or do anything. Forced energy takes twice the effort of natural energy. When you're in a state of fatigue, you use forced energy. By noon you're exhausted again!

When fatigue sets in, your highest priority should be to get rest. Eliminate any activities you can and just sleep as much as possible. You'll find that once you get rested, you'll again become positive and courageous, ready to face any challenge.

REST

Imagine going without sleep for twenty four hours or more and being challenged to a race or invited to try something new and exciting. You would be likely to decline the offer. When we're fatigued, everything seems overwhelming. Like Coach Lombardi says, we become "cowards" in such a condition. But after we get rested, the same challenges bring out our courageous and competitive side!

Maintaining a balance between rest, work, and play is very difficult to achieve in the teenage years, and is just as hard as an adult. When you find your parents getting irritable and negative, ask yourself, "Are they tired?" If so, encourage them. Help in ways which allow them to get some rest for a while, because often adults can't tell when they're fatigued any better than teenagers can!

In your teenage years fatigue may cause you to do poorly on a test or be grumpy on a date. In adulthood it may cause you to lose a major business deal or be rude to an important client. Try to recognize your own fatigue, without someone else having to point it out. Learn to rest when you are fatigued, because that's a skill you're going to need!

KEY QUESTIONS
1. *When do you most often tend to get fatigued?*
2. *How do you act when you're fatigued?*
3. *How do you feel after a good rest?*

ACTION POINT

If you are fatigued right now, make a plan to get as much sleep as you can get during the next seven days. Cancel any activities you're planning that aren't really vital. A week from now, check to see if you don't have a lot more natural energy when you get up in the morning.

"Who of you by worrying can add a single hour to his life? Since you cannot do this very little thing, why do you worry about the rest?"

(Luke 12:25, 26, NIV)

Passage suggested by Josh McDowell

Director, Josh McDowell Ministry, Dallas, Texas

As soon as you make a decision, a wide variety of questions may begin to worry you. You wonder, *Did I make the right choice? Am I going to go bankrupt? Will I look like a fool?* You may even wish you hadn't made the decision at all.

If your decision is an investment, you reduce the risk if you consult with wise advisers. Once you've done that and have actually gone through with the decision, don't spend a lot of time worrying about it afterward!

WHY WORRY?

Worry does no basic good at all. It puts your stomach in a knot, confuses your head, and gives you an unsettled feeling. One of the wisest things you can do when worry sets in is to simply pray, trust in God, and relax.

Remember: Everyone makes mistakes! There is not a person alive who has made a big decision who has not later felt he made a mistake. You can't do everything perfectly, so when you've made your decision, relax and don't worry too much about it.

The implications of Luke 12:25, 26 are that decisions involving money are only a small part of life. Be thankful you have your health, family, and future. If you make a bad decision—even if you lose a lot of money—it isn't going to make or break you. Simply pick yourself up and learn from losses and problems. But don't worry about things that are too late to correct or change.

HOW WILL THIS APPLY WHEN I'M ON MY OWN?

I have seen time and time again where adults invest in something or have financial worries, and it nearly "eats them alive." The person develops ulcers and worry habits, is nervous, fidgety, anxious, and can't concentrate on conversations—just because he is worried about money. Such behavior is unwise. Don't worry about *anything* to the extent that it destroys the rest of your life!

Anthony (Tony) Wauterlek, founder of the investment banking firm of Wauterlek and Brown in Chicago, has handled the investment of millions of dollars. He gives this advice about anxiety: "Be content with what you have, wherever you are, whatever you do, with how much in material gain God provides. For, 'in godliness with contentment, there is great gain.'"

KEY QUESTIONS

1. *Are you worrying about anything involving money? If not, what other areas in your life cause you to worry?*
2. *Do you really believe that worrying will make any difference? Will it add a dollar to your bank account or an hour to your life?*
3. *What happened the last time you worried so much? Didn't the situation turn out okay?*

ACTION POINT

Ask trusted advisers what steps you could take to overcome or reduce the worry in your life. Create a plan now to handle worry—especially in the area of finances—when you become an adult.

PRINCIPLE

52

Learn to look people in the eyes both when you listen to and when you talk to them!

I am one of the many people who find it difficult to look someone in the eye when talking to him or her. I find it fairly easy to maintain eye contact when I'm listening, but when I'm talking I frequently look away. Yet I know a lot of people distrust anyone who will not look them in the eye during a conversation.

LISTENING, TALKING, LOOKING
When you look a person in the eye you let him know, "I'm interested in what you're saying. I'm paying attention. I care about you." Listening carefully is a compliment to any individual.

The more you talk with people, the more you will begin to see there are 1001 subtle indicators of whether they are responding to what you're saying. It could be the twitch of an eye, the movement of their hands, or their facial gestures. Unless you look a person in the eye, it's difficult to get a feel for whether or not he is listening, if he agrees, or if he cares one way or the other about what you're saying.

HOW WILL THIS APPLY WHEN I'M ON MY OWN?
Few adults expect teenagers to have the patience for listening to their words or wisdom. You might even come to think that such attention isn't even important, but it is. You will find that you can really impress an adult if you'll simply listen carefully and look intensely into the person's eyes as you communicate.

162

And even if people don't expect much from teenagers, we assume adults should listen with intensity. When they don't, we take it as an insult. Here again, the quicker you can learn to listen intensely, speak clearly, and keep your eyes on the other person's eyes, the better your preparation for adulthood.

KEY QUESTIONS

1. *When you're talking to someone, how do you feel when he or she won't look you in the eye?*
2. *How do you think others feel when they are talking to you, but you won't look them in the eye?*
3. *Why do you think it's difficult to look someone in the eye? How might you work on overcoming that obstacle?*

ACTION POINT

During the next week, have at least three conversations where you do not allow your eyes to drift from the other person for more than a second or two at a time. Concentrate on maintaining eye contact both when you're talking and when you're listening.

CAREER

PRINCIPLES

Nothing is meaningful without a context or comparison.

PRINCIPLE

53

Is $1500 a steal for that car, or is it a rip-off?
Is Bethel College a good choice for me?
What does a score of 800 mean on an S.A.T. test?
What sweater should I buy next?

None of these questions can be answered until you have some kind of comparison. Until you know the "Blue Book" value of a car (which shows the suggested wholesale and retail prices), or you check with friends who have bought similar cars, you have no way of knowing whether it's a bargain or a bad deal.

Until you know which colleges you can get into and what the other schools are like, it's impossible to make a good decision as to whether or not Bethel College is a good school for you.

If you've never heard of the S.A.T. test, or don't know the requirements of the college you're interested in, you have no idea if a score of 800 is good or bad.

And unless you contrast the sweaters already in your closet with the one you want to buy, you can't make a good choice. You want to choose a new sweater that will complement all your other clothes.

FINDING THE MEANING
When I say that "nothing" is meaningful without a comparison, you may ask, "Isn't God meaningful without a context?" I would

point out, "It's in the context of the Bible that we begin to understand who He really is."

You may ask, "Isn't my relationship with my parents meaningful?" My answer is, "Yes, but it's in the context of your relationships with grandparents, friends, aunts and uncles, other people's parents, etc., that you begin to develop an appreciation for how meaningful your parents really are." Nothing is meaningful without a context.

The word "meaningful" is one of those that everyone seems to understand, yet is very difficult to describe. A simple definition of *meaning* is "something with value." How much something means to you depends on how valuable it is to you.

FOR EXAMPLE . . .

You make decisions nearly every day of your life. One of the best ways to avoid bad decisions is to establish some kind of comparison. When someone offers you a watch for $1000, you may say, "That's a rip-off because I can get a watch for $15." But suppose the watch is really valued at $2500! That makes it a steal! On the other hand, paying $100 for a watch may actually be a rip-off if it's only worth $5. As an adult, one of the things you must keep doing is deciding how meaningful something is before you make a decision about it. The better you get at putting things into context, the better your decisions will be.

Imagine going to a new restaurant and ordering a hamburger, french fries, and drink. When the waitress comes she brings what you ordered, and hands you a bill—for $25! You'd be furious! When she explains that hamburgers cost $20 at that restaurant, you might say, "Take this one back. I don't want it. It's not worth the price!" You could take such a bold stand because you could go to the restaurant next door and buy a hamburger just as good or better for $2 or so.

Now we'll change the setting a bit. Let's say your car breaks down fifty miles from nowhere in the middle of the desert. You haven't eaten for twenty four hours. You walk to a little restaurant and the only thing they have available is one hamburger, one order of french fries, and one can of pop left. This is the only restaurant within fifty miles, and the owner is stubborn. He says the only way he will sell you his last hamburger is if you'll pay $20 for it. Since this is an imaginary story, let's say you have $300 in your pocket. In that context, would you be willing to pay $20 for a hamburger?

Nothing is meaningful without a context or comparison. Whenever you buy something, establish as much context or comparison as you can, so you will get the best value for your money.

KEY QUESTIONS

1. *What major purchases will you be making in the next three to six months?*
2. *What are the primary sources for those items?*
3. *What other sources would your parents or friends know of that you could check out as well?*

ACTION POINT

Think of a decision you need to make that will require spending $50 to $100 during the next few weeks or months. Compare at least three sources of suppliers and see which is the best place to buy the item. Learn to experience the thrill of saving dollars or getting a better value for the same dollar by comparing and contrasting variables whenever you can.

PRINCIPLE

54

"Once the facts are clear, the decisions jump out at you."

Dr. Peter F. Drucker

As the president of a consulting firm, I deal with hundreds of decisions a year. Probably the most frequent mistake I see people commit is attempting to make decisions before the facts are clear. Until someone has considered all of his or her options, it's totally frustrating to try to make a decision about anything.

MAKING THE FACTS CLEAR

How do you get the facts? How do you know which facts to get? These were questions I struggled with as a young person. Probably the most basic and helpful questions are: Who? What? When? Where? Why? and How? (See Principle #21.) If you just answer these six questions, they will help you get the facts in any situation—such as buying a car. It's much easier to make a wise decision once you know things like:

- Who was the last owner?
- What are the wholesale and retail prices?
- What have other people paid recently for this model?
- When was the last time a mechanic checked the car?
- When will they expect payment?
- Where might I get a better deal?
- Why is the car being sold?
- How much do I have in the bank?
- How much do they want for the car?

DECISIONS JUMP OUT AT YOU

Making decisions is an everyday part of life. As you grow into adulthood, decisions get larger. The better you become at making decisions today, the wiser your decisions will be as an adult.

Suppose you have $1500 to buy a car. Three cars are advertised in the local newspaper in your price range, so you call each of the numbers. The first car has 150,000 miles and has never been overhauled. The second has a brand-new engine and tires, but the price has been raised to $1700. The third car is the same make and model as the others, has only 20,000 miles on it, has had the best of treatment, and costs $1400. In fact, it's even a color you like better.

If you had bought the first car you called about, do you see how you would have lost out? If you took the second one, you'd spend too much money and still not have the best car. By collecting and clarifying all the facts, your decisions become obvious.

KEY QUESTIONS

1. *What are the top three decisions you need to make in the next three to six months?*
2. *What facts do you need for each of them, in order for the decisions to jump out?*
3. *Do you have at least three options in each case?*

ACTION POINT

For each of the decisions you need to make, begin to accumulate facts. Start now so you will have as much time as possible in making each decision.

PRINCIPLE

55

"Efficiency is doing things right. Effectiveness is doing right things."

DR. PETER F. DRUCKER

An important part of living successfully on your own is learning how to be both effective and efficient. It is not enough to be only efficient. For example, suppose a teacher assigns 30 pages of reading. You can read the first three pages over and over again, and you can do it efficiently, with no distractions, and giving it your full attention. Yet no matter how efficiently you read those three pages, your time won't have been used effectively because you will know nothing about the other 27 pages.

If you need to paint the four walls of your room, it is ineffective to paint the same wall four times. Even though you work just as hard, it doesn't get the job done. Efficiency is doing things right. Effectiveness is doing right things.

DOING THINGS RIGHT

Everyone wants to do things right. But when the focus becomes doing one thing to excess while other necessary jobs are left undone, you have a problem with efficiency. Having high standards is good, but being driven by perfectionism can be destructive. If you feel you must be perfect in order to be accepted, talk with your parents or your pastor to find out why you feel that way.

DOING RIGHT THINGS

Because I am president of a consulting firm, many people assume I do a lot of time management seminars where they can learn how to save 10 minutes here and 20 minutes there. A lot of people are surprised to discover that's not what I teach. You can waste 10 minutes here, and an hour there—even a day now and then—and still get a tremendous amount done in a year. If, when you work, you work on the right things, you still get a lot done!

One of my favorite bits of advice is, "Decide what to say no to." Deciding what you really want to get done and then sticking with it is a key to doing the right things. (See Principle #58.)

The older you get, the more you will see the value of this principle. Many adults stay so busy trying to "do things right" that they neglect to "do right things." As my friend Loren Lillestrand says, they "get so busy selling the peanuts, they forget to watch the game." Learn to maintain a balance in your life of doing things right *and* doing right things.

Imagine you're out walking in a field when you come across a guy using a 72" McCulloch chain saw to cut down underbrush—though the chainsaw is capable of cutting down giant redwood trees. You stop and ask, "What are you doing there, friend?"

He screams over the sound of the powerful, noisy chainsaw, "I'm cutting underbrush to build a house! I've gotten so efficient, I can cut more underbrush per hour than any person alive! I designed a machine that bundles it and stacks it beside the road, where a forklift loads it onto a truck! I have 53,000 loads of it ready to go!"

You yell back, "Why are you sawing all these brush bundles?"

"To build me a log cabin," is his short reply.

You point out that log cabins aren't built with underbrush. Rather, they're built with pine trees.The man says, "You mean I've been working for 14 years cutting down underbrush, and I still don't have what I need to build a house? I've worked 18 hours a day, 7 days a week, and I still can't build a cabin?"

He shuts off his saw and you say in what seems like a whisper, "Nope. You've got a real efficient system there, but you haven't been cutting down the right stuff." So he begins to cut down pine trees, and in three days he has collected enough to build his house.

As you strive to be efficient in the things you do, don't forget to be effective as well.

KEY QUESTIONS

1. *What are three realistic and measurable goals you have for the next 90 days?*

2. *What are some things you could eliminate in order to be more effective in reaching your goals?*

3. *What three trusted people could you discuss your goals with, to make sure these are the right goals to be pursuing?*

ACTION POINT

What three things do you most want to accomplish this year? Go over your thoughts with parents or close friends. You have now taken the first step toward effectiveness. You may waste time, but if you get the three major things done, you will still have made a lot of progress!

Leadership is knowing what to do next, knowing why that's important, and knowing how to bring the appropriate resources to bear on the need at hand.

PRINCIPLE

56

"Am I a leader?" "Will I ever be a leader?" "Is everyone supposed to be a leader?"

These questions probably go through every teenager's mind at least once. I remember being frustrated about not knowing exactly how to define a leader. I couldn't tell if I was a leader or not. There were times I wanted to lead, but other people didn't seem to recognize my leadership. Sometimes I *didn't* want to be the leader, but others seemed to expect me to lead. Frankly, it was a very confusing subject until I was in my early 20s.

One of the breakthroughs for me was defining leadership. You will hear a lot of definitions of leadership over the years, but you'll find there is not a single, agreed-upon, adult definition of leadership. The sooner you find a definition of leadership you feel comfortable with, the easier it will be to decide about your own leadership abilities.

KNOW WHAT TO DO NEXT

Often you may find yourself in a group situation where no one seems to know what to do next. No one will take the initiative to make a decision. You'll find that whoever can suggest what to do next, and have the group go along with it, begins to emerge as leader.

If you are ever chosen as president of your class or leader of your youth group, spend most of your time trying to answer the question, "What shall we do next?" Or as my friend Steve Douglass,

Executive Vice President of Campus Crusade for Christ, asks: "What three things can we do in the next 30 to 90 days that will make a 50 percent difference . . . or get us 50 percent of the way to our goal?"

For example, if you're in the process of raising money for a class trip, ask yourself, *What three things could our class do in the next 30 to 60 days to raise half of the money we need?* If you keep your thinking focused on "What do we do next?" you'll be surprised how effective you can be as a leader.

Incidentally, all the ideas do not have to come from you. Have group discussions with your friends and brainstorm lots of ideas. But whoever focuses on what the whole group, class, or troop should do next will begin to emerge as the leader.

KNOW WHY

A lot of people come up with good ideas, but can't explain them in ways the group can easily understand and endorse. Spend plenty of time thinking through reasons why a particular idea is right. Don't give suggestions "off the top of your head" to get the group to go along. If you want to provide real leadership, decide what you feel is right to do next, then prepare to explain why to the group.

By the way, it's far easier to get a group to do something if you are meeting a need they feel. If they are hungry, it's pretty easy to convince them to go down to the local restaurant. If they're not hungry, going to a restaurant won't make as much sense to them.

BRING APPROPRIATE RESOURCES

A "resource" can be money, people, ideas, equipment, tools, or anything necessary to get the job done. If you can say, "Here's what we need to do next and here's why it's important," while providing whatever is needed, you are providing solid leadership.

SPIRITUAL LEADERSHIP

A logical question at this point is: "How does regular leadership differ from spiritual leadership?" Spiritual leadership is simply:

Knowing what Jesus would do next,

Knowing why He would do that, and,
Knowing how to bring whatever resources *He* would bring
to bear on the need at hand.

Spiritual leadership is simply looking at leadership from Christ's perspective. Instead of money or equipment, Jesus often responded to the need at hand by praying to His Father.

GIVE IT A TRY

A lot of times you'll find yourself in a position where you don't know whether or not to try to lead a group. Before you say anything, ask yourself, "Do I know what to do next? Can I explain why I would want to do it? And do I know how to bring resources together to get this job done?" If you can't answer yes to these questions, it might be better to stand back and let someone else lead. But if you have good answers for them, go ahead and try it!

The following imaginary story illustrates this leadership definition:

One evening a plane lifted off the runway at John F. Kennedy Airport in New York City. On the plane, headed for an international business congress in the gleaming South American city of Brasilia, were 374 presidents of Fortune 500 companies.

The only exception to the distinguished list of business and industrial leaders was a special guest of the United Nations, an Amazon jungle chieftain. This had been the chief's first visit to the civilized world, and it was certainly the business executives' first encounter with anyone like him.

The ten-hour flight was interrupted 600 miles north of Brasilia, right in the heart of the Amazon jungle, when the plane developed major engine trouble and made an emergency landing in a large clearing. The passengers were 200 miles from the closest village.

No one was injured, but as the passengers all stepped out into the steamy jungle, with its exotic birds, chattering monkeys, poisonous berries, quicksand, and pythons, can you guess who began to provide leadership for the group? Yes, it was the jungle chieftain. He was the only passenger who knew:

What to do next (in a jungle),

Why he would do what needed to be done, and

How to bring appropriate resources (such as fresh water and nonpoisonous berries) to bear on the need at hand.

KEY QUESTIONS

1. *In what area would you most like to be an effective leader?*
2. *What three things should the group do in the next one to three months?*
3. *Why would you suggest each of these steps, and what resources would your group need in order to take these steps?*

ACTION POINT

Focus on the one area where you would most like to provide leadership. Spend a few minutes thinking about what you'd like to do next, why you would do it, and what resources you could bring.

When things seem overwhelming, make a list of all the things you've got to do, put them in order of importance, and start at the top.

PRINCIPLE

57

It's my guess that every single person in the world has thought, *I'll never get caught up. . . . It's hopeless. . . . I'm so far behind, I don't know where to begin!* We all know that overwhelmed feeling of having so many things to do we don't even know where to start!

MAKE A LIST
When you begin to feel buried by all the things you need to do, ask yourself, *What do I have to do by the end of today? By the end of the week? By the end of the month?* Put a time limit on the things you need to accomplish.

Let your mind dump onto a piece of paper all the things you feel pressured to accomplish in the near future, and form a list. Making a list of things to do is about as sensible to me as making a grocery list when going to the market. When items are listed on a sheet of paper, you don't forget anything, you can organize what you need to do, and you have the satisfaction of crossing off each item as it is accomplished. Begin to see lists as friends, not enemies.

IN ORDER OF IMPORTANCE
If your list is long, you may feel overwhelmed and not know where to begin. That's when you make a second list! Ask yourself, *If I could only do one thing, which one would I do?* That thing becomes number one on your new list. Then ask, *If I got number one done and could only do one other thing, what would I do?* That becomes number

two . . . and so on. This little bit of extra planning is valuable because it makes sure you're getting the highest priorities done first.

START AT THE TOP

Start at the top of your list whenever possible, but there may be occasional exceptions. Sometimes you may feel too discouraged, overwhelmed, or fatigued to tackle the number one task—especially if it is a big one. You may want to start with a couple of easy items and check them off to feel like you're making progress. Just do something! If you keep "chipping away" at the list and checking off items, sooner or later they are all done!

For my senior year of college I transferred from Bethel (a small Christian college with about 500 students) to Michigan State University (with a campus of 35,000). The first day I was absolutely overwhelmed! I soon had thousands of pages to read, stringent course requirements to meet, and more than I thought I would ever be able to handle. I remember thinking, *I'm going to have this overwhelmed feeling hundreds of times in my life. How do I deal with it?* That's how I discovered the value of making lists.

Three years later I completed my Bachelors and then my Masters at Michigan State. Since then I've faced a lot of overwhelming times, but I've never forgotten the feeling of relief that came from simply making a list . . . and starting somewhere!

KEY QUESTIONS

1. *What are all the things you need to do?*
2. *What is the order of importance of those things?*
3. *What are the top three things you could do in the next seven days?*

ACTION POINT

Get a piece of paper and a pencil. Write out all the things you need to do—call Jami, talk to Joli, write Evida, finish studying for my English test, take my geometry test, and so forth. If you make the list and do one thing at a time, you won't feel nearly as overwhelmed. "Keep on keeping on," and sooner or later you will be done!

"Deciding what *not* to do is just as important as deciding what to do."

ARCHIE B. PARRISH

PRINCIPLE

58

Lots of people come to me as the president of a consulting firm, and ask, "Bobb, could you teach a time-management seminar?" They want to keep track of where their time goes and learn how to spend it more efficiently. Without meaning to downplay the value of using time wisely I often tell them, "No, I'm not quite as interested in saving ten minutes here and there as I used to be. What I'm more interested in is deciding what *not* to do!"

You see, by just deciding *not* to serve on one board, I can save literally days a year. Deciding *not* to write one book may save 300 hours in a given year. Deciding *not* to go on a vacation could give me two weeks in a year to do something else. Deciding what *not* to do is more important than you might think! I would rather spend 15 minutes trying to decide what not to do than trying to figure out how I could do *everything* quicker, better, and more efficiently.

DECIDING WHAT TO ELIMINATE

It is important to decide what needs to be done, and to prioritize those things. (See Principle #57.) I like to ask myself four questions:

    (1) If I could only do three things, what would I do?

    (2) What would Jesus do if He were here?

    (3) If I could only do one important thing in the next seven days, what would I do?

    (4) If I could only do one thing this entire year, what single thing would I most want to do?

By asking those kinds of questions, you can sort out what you have to do and want to do. You also determine the things you can say *no* to.

HOW WILL THIS APPLY WHEN I'M ON MY OWN?

The need to prioritize your schedule intensifies as you begin to do more things on your own. The better you get now at deciding what *not* to do, the more effective you'll become.

I have heard that Napoleon could write letters to two different friends, on different topics, with both hands going at the same time! I find that difficult to believe. He may have been writing letters on different topics to two friends, but he would likely write to one friend for a sentence or two, and then to the other one for a sentence or two. His mind must have been concentrating on one friend or the other at any single point in time.

I bring this up simply to show that while you're doing one thing, it's very difficult to focus your attention on another. Some people are very good at "killing two birds with one stone," such as doing needlepoint and watching television simultaneously. But typically, people do only one thing a time. You can't spend the same hour watching television and studying for finals at the same time—not with the same results as if you focused only on studying. Since everything is ultimately a trade-off, it is important to decide what you really want to do, and what you want to say no to.

By simply eliminating one or two nonessential things, you can concentrate on the three or four things you absolutely must get done. Every hour of your life is an investment—every hour of sleep, every hour of work, every hour of play, every hour of conversation. Learn to ask yourself, "Is this the best investment I can make toward the future I want to have?"

KEY QUESTIONS

1. *What are your top 10 priorities for the next 30 to 90 days?*
2. *In what order of importance or priority would you do these 10 things?*
3. *What could you stop doing for a while to give yourself adequate time to accomplish the other items on your list?*

ACTION POINT

Make a list of the 10 things you would most like to accomplish in the next 30 days. Put them in order of importance. Then ask yourself: "Is anything on this list that I could get by without doing? Am I involved in other activities not on this list that I could eliminate in order to get these things done? Could I postpone any of these things for a while?" As you identify nonessential areas, don't be afraid to say, "I'm sorry, I just can't do it at this time."

Everyone must take risks, but planning and research helps reduce the number of unnecessary and unwise risks you take.

PRINCIPLE

59

Some decisions you have to make are not that tough. If you decide to take French instead of Spanish and later discover that Spanish would have been more useful, you may wish you had chosen differently. But you haven't really lost out on anything.

Other decisions are more risky. "Should we buy this house?" "Should we move the company to another state?" "Should I start my own business?" If you make the wrong decision on questions like these, you could lose a lot of time or money. Throughout life you will be faced by questions that involve a high amount of risk.

Being conservative does not mean you don't take risks. Playing it safe doesn't mean you don't take risks. Every person alive, sooner or later, has to take risks. The only options are how you approach the risk, and the size of the risk you take.

MINIMIZING RISK
By simply doing a little planning and research, you will reduce the number of unnecessary and unwise risks you make. Planning helps you anticipate where problems will occur. Look ahead and ask, "How much money will we have to invest at each step?" Know the facts, but remember that any major project still contains a certain amount of risk.

Some people enjoy taking major risks. They do their homework to determine the possibilities and then plunge into promising new endeavors. Other people don't feel comfortable taking risks until all the research is completed and double-checked twice! (This is something to keep in mind as you choose a life partner in marriage. It's one of the areas you should discuss thoroughly. If you are uncomfortable at taking risks and your mate is a "high roller," your differences may create major friction.)

One time I can remember taking something of a major risk was while I was on staff at World Vision, an organization that helps people in underdeveloped countries. Perhaps you have seen a "Love Loaf." It's a small money container in the shape of a loaf of bread with a fish on top, representing the loaves and fishes Jesus multiplied to feed hungry people. I designed and developed the Love Loaf program, so I had the responsibility of supervising the amount of risk we took in developing the idea. During the first year, I invested a lot of World Vision's money to pay for literature, manufacturing, advertising, etc. Our expenses were considerably more than we took in. The risk was pretty large.

Then the program started to turn around, and has since raised millions of dollars to reduce world hunger. But it required a risk to invest money in the first place. All of our study did not eliminate the risk. It simply eliminated other unnecessary and unwise decisions we might have taken.

WATCH OUT!

I should offer a word of warning at this point. Whenever you consider taking a risk, beware of "too good to be true" schemes. Here's a popular one among con artists:

First someone convinces you to invest a small amount of money (maybe $100) in some area where he is an expert, promising to double your money within a week. This person usually says he is investing his own money as well. When the week passes, he gives back your $100 *plus* another $200. He says, "This worked out great! If I get other deals, do you want to be in on them?" You'll probably say yes.

In two weeks he returns and says, "I've got another opportunity for you. It will require $1000 from you, but I can get you back $5000 within a month!" Since this investment is also in an area where he's an expert, you hand over the money. At the end of the month, he gives you the $5000. By now you think the guy's a financial wizard!

Then comes the real setup. He tells you of a deal where it's practically guaranteed that he can make you a million dollars—if you'll invest pretty much everything you have in your life savings! (This time it happens to be an area he knows hardly anything about, but you tend to trust his judgment because he has "proven" himself.) That's when he takes you for all you've got! He takes the money and later tells you, "I'm sorry, but we just got wiped out. There's no money left."

When you're going to take a risk, make sure it's in an area of *your* expertise. Or ask someone you know and trust personally (someone *not* involved in the deal), who is an expert. For example, before you choose a school, have someone (perhaps your school counselor), check into the school and make sure it's a wise match for you. As you reduce the level of risk involved in any decision, you increase the likelihood of your satisfaction in the future.

KEY QUESTIONS
1. *What are some risks you're about to take that could be costly?*
2. *What planning or research could you do to reduce the number of unnecessary and unwise risks you take?*
3. *With what person could you discuss the risk in order to get an additional perspective?*

ACTION POINT
Think of a purchase you are considering that will be more than $50. Before buying the item, do some "research" by checking three other sources to see if you can find a better deal. Also take time to get the perspective of someone else who has made a similar purchase, or who knows a lot about the product you're considering.

Ultimately you can break every system into four steps: Input, Process, Output, and Feedback.

PRINCIPLE

60

When you have a big job to do, do you ever wonder: *Where do I start? What do I do next? What am I expecting to get done? How will I know if I'm on track? How do I do it most efficiently?* Whenever you're trying to do any big job, or run any kind of program or organization, you can break down the work flow into four areas: Input, Process, Output, and Feedback. Here are some examples.

Example #1—You're the student manager of an ice-cream shop.

INPUT—Everything you do to get customers into the shop, such as advertising, window displays, free coupons, etc.

PROCESS—What customers experience from the time they come in until they receive what they came for (the ice cream).

OUTPUT—The quality of the ice-cream cone itself. Is the ice cream old and refrozen, or is it fresh and delicious?

FEEDBACK—Customer responses to the ice cream. They might tell their friends about it; they may fill out a questionnaire about it; or they may become repeat customers!

Example #2—You're the president of the youth group at church.

INPUT—New people coming into the group.

PROCESS—What they experience from the time they arrive at the door until they leave.

OUTPUT—What people learn and take away from the meeting.

FEEDBACK—People's responses to the meeting.

Example #3—You're the principal of a local high school.

INPUT—Students coming into the school.

PROCESS—The courses they take.

OUTPUT—Your graduates.

FEEDBACK—Comments by graduates, such as, "When I got out into the real world, I discovered you didn't teach me the right things," or, "I really benefited from your class."

No matter what you're doing—starting your own business, learning a new job, teaching someone a new skill, or whatever—ultimately every job can be broken down into these four steps. Once you see how they work, it's pretty easy to organize your thinking in any area.

PROCESS CHARTING

Breaking things down into steps could be shown as follows:

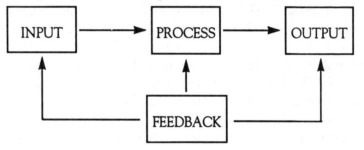

As you get farther along in using process design, you'll find that even major systems can be broken into small steps to show how they work. It's a lot like the diagram for wiring a stereo that shows where all the wires go. That is basically a process chart or system. Start using lines and boxes to show how your thinking is developing on a project.

For example: Let's say you wanted to show how you were going to plan a family vacation. It might look something like this:

$$\boxed{1} \rightarrow \boxed{2} \rightarrow \boxed{3} \rightarrow \boxed{4} \rightarrow \boxed{5} \rightarrow \boxed{6} \rightarrow \boxed{7}$$

Step 1: Decide where we're going to go.
Step 2: Get the car ready.
Step 3: Pack the car.
Step 4: Go on vacation.
Step 5: Write postcards to everyone while on vacation.
Step 6: Return home.
Step 7: Unpack car and return to normal life.

This is an oversimplification of a process chart, but it's easy to take each of those squares and break it down into its subparts. For example, "Step 3: Pack the car," could break down like this:

A. Pack our clothes.
B. Pack our equipment.
C. Pack our food.
D. Pack whatever else we need.

HOW WILL THIS APPLY WHEN I'M ON MY OWN?

You may be asked to plan many events. If you're responsible for planning a party, you must deal with publicity, decorations, food, transportation, entertainment, recreation, gifts, and "big-bang" ending.

Anything you ever need to plan can be put into a systematic, step-by-step process. Once you know what the 10 to 30 steps are in planning a party, vacation, or start-up company, it's fairly easy to lay out the process in terms of input, process, output, and feedback.

I have a friend who was an engineer at Bell Laboratories in the 1960s when NASA did the moon shot. He told me there were hundreds of engineers and thousands of suppliers. Everything had to come together to put the rocket on the moon and bring it back again. The operation would not have been possible without a systems approach. Ultimately the moon shot could be broken down into:

Prepare rocket.
Launch rocket.
Orbit moon.
Return to earth.
Land.
Debrief astronauts.

Every category probably had thousands of considerations. But by using this basic process, no plan is too complex.

Process charting is easy for some and hard for others. If you find it difficult, watch someone else do it or recruit someone on your team who finds it easy. And if it comes naturally to you, don't assume everyone else finds it as easy as you do.

KEY QUESTIONS
1. *What things do you have to plan this year?*
2. *What are the 10 to 30 steps required to accomplish each plan?*
3. *Who can help you make sure you've covered all the areas properly? Who has done it before?*

ACTION POINT
Think of an upcoming event that needs to be planned in the next six months. Then work through the four-step process. What are the basic steps involved? What is the input? What are the process steps? How can you ensure happy "customers"? What is the output you need? What are you hoping will be the final outcome? How will people let you know what they liked or disliked about what you did?

Try your hand at laying out the plan in an orderly, organized way and then following through on it.

Invest your time wisely. Spend 80 percent of the time where you are the strongest, 15 percent on learning new things, and 5 percent in areas where you need or want to grow.

PRINCIPLE

61

There's an old school of thought which says you should concentrate on your weaknesses until you overcome them. I disagree. Instead, I encourage you to concentrate on your strengths and become even better at what you do best. After you gain confidence from being good at something, then you can move on to areas where you don't feel as confident. Occasionally take on an area where you feel downright insecure. But if you spend most of your time in areas where you feel insecure, it will ultimately destroy your self-confidence.

FOCUS ON YOUR STRENGTHS

When you're young, time seems to go very slowly. The older you get, the faster time seems to pass. Invest your time wisely, because soon you'll have many additional responsibilities.

Until you're about 30 years old, concentrate a lot of time on finding out what you're really good at, what you enjoy most, what you find easy that most people find difficult. In short, discover where your strengths lie. In junior high, it's very difficult to know your real strengths. You try a lot of different things. Someday you may be a classical composer, but you haven't taken your first music lesson yet!

While you're under thirty, don't worry a lot about failing. When you try new things, you're going to fail sometimes. Besides, you've still got plenty of time to overcome early failures in life. One of the problems in our society is that we pressure young people too soon

191

to decide what they're going to do in life. Kids are asked at age 4 or 5 to decide if they want to be Olympic athletes. People in junior high have to start thinking about college. In high school you're supposed to decide on a career. To a large extent, we have no idea what we want to do until we're in our twenties.

However, education is one thing you *do* need to complete as soon as you can. Once you're married and have children, it's very difficult to go back to school. But it isn't critical to know by age 21 exactly what you plan to do with the rest of your life, even if you've graduated from college. Many people truly don't know!

If you do know, so much the better. Some young people decide to be doctors based on a love of medicine, chemistry, physics, anatomy, etc. That's fine for them, but it might not be right for you. Be cautious. Before you decide to be a doctor, watch a doctor for a while. Before you decide to be an accountant, watch an accountant.

It's no tragedy to be 23 years old and still not know precisely what you want to do with your life. The tragedy is being 37, and realizing you made the wrong choice. It typically takes a few years to define your primary strengths. But keep asking, "What do I enjoy most? What am I really best at?" Spend 80 percent of your time in those areas.

NEW THINGS AND AREAS OF GROWTH

After you become confident you can do something exceptionally well, begin to spend about 15 percent of your time trying new things you think you might enjoy, but aren't sure. Also spend five percent of your time experimenting with areas you've never seriously considered. For example: You may eat foods you enjoy 80 percent of the time, try new foods that look appealing 15 percent of the time, and experiment with the other five percent of your diet, trying foods from other countries, delicacies, gourmet foods, or health food.

A word of caution: Some things are clearly wrong and danger-ous, and should be left alone *100 percent of the time*. For example, you should never experiment with drugs. Even a five percent experimentation can quickly get you hooked to where you'll soon be spending 80 percent of your time (and money) doing drugs.

There is so much to experiment with in life without becoming involved with things like drugs. I encourage you to experiment with foods, activities, clothing styles, and new experiences that will help you discover what you really enjoy and are good at.

KEY QUESTIONS

1. How can you arrange your life to spend most of your time doing what you're best at (your 80 percent areas)?
2. What are some things you would like to experiment with (your 15 percent areas)?
3. This year, what entirely new things would you like to try (your five percent areas)?

ACTION POINT

Ask a few adults how happy they are in their work. Ask if they would choose the same career if they had it to do over again. See how they decided on the professions they're in, and whether they have ever tried other things. For those who are unhappy, ask how they made the mistake of choosing the wrong career. Their responses will give you perspective when you need to get serious about determining your career.

A picture is worth a thousand words . . . and a graph or chart is worth ten thousand numbers.

Every time you pick up a magazine, a newspaper, or a company's annual report, you tend to look first at the pictures, pie charts, line graphs, bar charts, etc.

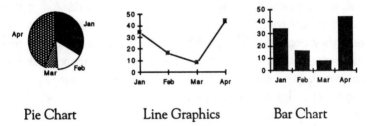

Pie Chart   Line Graphics   Bar Chart

Just as it might take 1500 words to describe the victorious smile of an Olympic champion who has just won a gold medal, it would take ten thousand numbers to explain what a few simple graphics can show in a matter of seconds.

SEEING AND UNDERSTANDING
Some people understand things best by hearing them, but most of us do better when we see them. Graphics help your presentation whether you're advertising a school play, selling a used car, or running for a student government office.

One of the things you should learn as soon as possible is how to translate statistics into chart or graph form. This is not something that comes easily at first, but with practice you can do it. It is especially important to get good with graphs and charts if you go into any profession which requires presentations to be made. Today's computer graphics software packages make it much easier to create professional-looking charts and graphs than it used to be.

A lot of people find it very difficult to understand numbers. I'm one of those people. I find it hard to read a financial statement with columns of numbers, especially if I can't see all the numbers at one time. But if I see the information in the form of a chart, I am able to understand the whole picture at a glance!

If you ever need to make presentations, perhaps to convince people to invest money or take financial risks based on your ideas, you are likely to overwhelm them if you just throw out a lot of numbers. They will feel anxious and insecure in taking the next step you're suggesting. But if you can communicate the same information with graphs and charts, they are much more likely to be interested in your cause—and do what you ask of them!

KEY QUESTIONS
1. *What numbers do you need to understand?*
2. *Would a pie chart, a line graph, or a bar chart help you better understand how you are doing financially?*
3. *Do your parents keep any charts or graphs? If so, discuss the visual material with them.*

ACTION POINT
Make a single line chart of your income projections (what you expect to receive each month) for the next year. Then keep track to see how close you come.

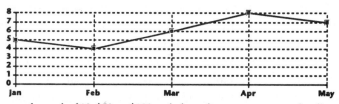

Income

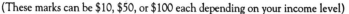

(These marks can be $10, $50, or $100 each depending on your income level)

195

PRINCIPLE

63

An activity is only work when you'd rather be doing something else.

I tell people I retired at age 34, even though I've been consulting full-time since then. Most of them know there are very few things I'd rather be doing than consulting. I would enjoy it even if I didn't get paid!

You will know you have found an ideal career when you discover you are excited about going to work each day! You won't watch the hands of the clock all the time. An old German proverb says, "The hands of the clock stand still only for those who are bored at work."

TAKING THE WORK OUT OF YOUR JOB

Any activities you do when you'd rather be doing something else seem like real chores—even things that should be fun. But when you finally find a job that pays a salary for doing what you would want to do anyway, it will seem more like play than work!

If you have a job scooping cones at an ice-cream shop, but you'd rather be fixing motorcycles at a garage, you're not going to be very happy at work. You may have trouble showing up on time, doing the best job you can, or finding creative ways of improving service at the ice-cream shop. If you're a waitress but you'd rather be working in a dress shop, you'll just be putting in your time and watching the hands on the clock until your shift comes to an end.

But if you're working at a job you enjoy, you will be excited and challenged to learn new things. You'll find it easy to do a good job. You'll impress your employer with your enthusiasm and the good ideas you have. You'll be promoted! Each day you'll look forward to getting to work. You'll be surprised at how quickly it's quitting time! When you consider the number of hours you will spend at a job, it makes sense to direct your energy toward something you will enjoy.

HOW WILL THIS APPLY WHEN I'M ON MY OWN?
It is my estimate that 60 percent of all adults are not happy at work. The freeway is full of bumper stickers that say so: "I'd rather be flying," "I'd rather be surfing." "I'd rather be skiing."

If you'd rather be at the beach all the time, why not be a lifeguard? If you enjoy working with numbers, why not be an accountant? Find something you enjoy so much, you'd do it whether or not you got paid for it. That can point you toward a career you'll still be enjoying when you're 65.

Sure, sometimes the need to make enough money to pay for a car, clothes, etc., will dictate your career choices. But if you're 35, 45, or 55, and are still doing just what you have to do to pay the bills, then you should rethink your position.

Now is the time to concentrate on this principle. As you get out into the adult world, you will be ready to take the steps necessary to choose a career you enjoy.

KEY QUESTIONS
1. *How would you enjoy making a living that would not seem like "work"?*
2. *Do your parents enjoy their work? Why or why not?*
3. *What are the things you would absolutely never want to do as a career? Why?*

ACTION POINT
Make a list of all the things you enjoy. Then consider all careers that involve your list of activities. Making this list will be helpful and insightful to you, particularly if you discuss it with your parents.

"Whatever profession you go into, it's good to pick something that looks real interesting. Get the right education, and go for it!"

J. IRA BIEHL—AUTHOR, CONSTRUCTION WORKER, AND STUDENT
HOLLYWOOD, CALIFORNIA

Whenever you feel negative about school, remember this principle. Decide what you think you really want to do, find a school that prepares you for it, get the right education, and go for it!

Learn to appreciate your teachers. They are there to teach you to perform in a certain profession. They can be frustrating if they are teaching a subject you don't like, but education is sort of like a union card or permit to work; you have to have it to get certain jobs.

When you're going to school you can't see what education is going to do for you, because you're just trying to graduate. But once you get out, you begin to realize what your teachers were trying to do. Take advantage of your education, because it will prepare you for better jobs in the long run. Decide what you think you want to do, go get the right education, and try it!

Think of yourself as a lifelong student—not afraid of education, but eager to learn new things that will help you do your job better! Think of education not as something you have to put up with, but as something valuable that will give you knowledge and background to succeed in your chosen profession.

HOW WILL THIS APPLY WHEN I'M ON MY OWN?

Recently a computer programmer friend said, "I've worked in the computer business now for 21 years. I've worked on 23 very different systems because of the advancement of the technology. I'm always in school!"

Beginning in about 1970, the turnover in adult employment

caused educators to say that before you reached retirement you likely would be retrained three or four times for different occupations. Today, you may find that your educational preparation takes three or four years. Even then, you may have to go back to school for additional training.

KEY QUESTIONS

1. *What interests do you have now that you might like to have as a job when you are 30 years old?*
2. *What kind of education would it take to get ready for such a job?*
3. *What people can help you discover what education you need and help you get into the right schools (universities, trade schools, evening courses, etc.) to prepare for the job you want?*

ACTION POINT

Between now and the time you are 30, you may change your mind 15 times about your profession. But for right now, complete the following sentence:

"By the time I am 30, I would like to be a _____. In order to be qualified for that position, I would need to go through the following educational program:_____.
The person I know who has a position like this is _____, and in the next 30 days I will talk to him or her about the position. I will also see if I can watch him or her at work doing what I think I want to do by the time I'm 30."

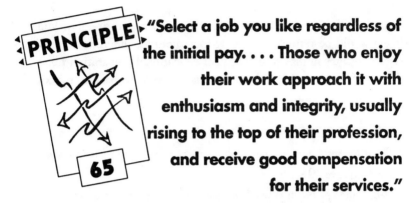

"Select a job you like regardless of the initial pay. . . . Those who enjoy their work approach it with enthusiasm and integrity, usually rising to the top of their profession, and receive good compensation for their services."

LEE EATON—PRESIDENT, EATON FARMS, INCORPORATED, LEXINGTON, KENTUCKY

My son J. really likes this principle. (It's similar to Principle #64, which he created.) J.'s friend Lisa works at a supermarket. People who work there get a raise after a certain amount of time. If they stick with it, they're given good jobs in the meat department or the deli. If they like the people they work with, eventually they can be making $20 an hour in the butcher department. If you take a job you like, even though you don't make much money at first, five years down the line you might be running the place.

LIKE WHAT YOU DO

One of the first temptations you are likely to face on your own is to take any job that pays a lot. Unfortunately, many people get trapped into staying in jobs they don't like simply because the pay continues to increase. At the upper-executive level in major companies, senior executives refer to these trapped feelings as being in "golden handcuffs." They feel bound, but they like the gold!

Obviously, the younger you are, the less choice you have in the kinds of jobs available to you. But as you get into your late teens, begin to select jobs you like rather than ones you do just for the money. As soon as you can, find a job or profession you really enjoy.

Let's say you have two employment opportunities. The one you like better pays 50 cents an hour less than the other one. But take the one you enjoy. You will be much more excited about it. Sooner or later you will get a promotion and the pay will go up as well.

HOW WILL THIS APPLY WHEN I'M ON MY OWN?

Many adults are "stuck" in jobs they don't enjoy. The person feels the position "brings home the bacon," but provides very little personal satisfaction, fulfillment, or success. The majority of these adults would jump at the chance to start over in life, possibly stay in school longer, or pursue a different career. But now they make so much money that they can't start over in a career they enjoy and still make enough to pay for the house, the car, and their other bills.

That's why it's crucial for you to begin now to look for jobs in areas that you enjoy doing.

Of course, there isn't a job in the world where you won't have a bad day occasionally. Just because you go through a day or two (or even a week or two) of depression or discouragement in your job doesn't mean it's not for you. However, if you experience weeks and months of frustration at work, find an alternative job and give it a try. You may discover that the new job isn't any better. Or you may find that it is exactly what you needed.

The bottom line is to do something that you like and can get excited about. Be honest on the job, do the best you possibly can, and chances are you will rise to a major position of responsibility in a position you truly enjoy.

KEY QUESTIONS

1. *If you could have any job in the world today, realistically, what job would you most like to have?*
2. *If you could work with any person in the world, who would it be?*
3. *What amount of money would you like to make someday? Is it realistic to make that amount of money in the field you are considering?*

ACTION POINT

Ask two or three adults who know you fairly well (perhaps your parents) what kind of positions they think you would enjoy and be good at. Begin to get a feel for what your options are. Imagine what you might enjoy doing and begin developing a plan to get there.

"Most of your business opportunities or career positions will be obtained through personal contacts. Now is the time for you to develop a personal network."

Loren Miller—Vice President and Treasurer
Hershey Oil Corporation, Pasadena, California

One of life's realities is that employers tend to hire people they know. They frequently give special consideration to friends and children of friends.

This certainly does not mean that you can't get a job if you don't know the manager or president of a company. Neither does it mean that if you know the president you are guaranteed a position. However, if you *do* know the president, the chances are better of getting a job than if you don't know him or her.

IT NEVER HURTS TO ASK

Incidentally, there is nothing wrong with asking your friends if they know about position openings. Over 50 percent of all the jobs in the country are filled by friends of current employees. This seems to work better than classified ads, employment agencies, or other ways of finding positions. Therefore, it's a very effective way to find work. If you are looking for work, don't be afraid to ask all your friends, "Do you know of any positions that will be opening up soon?"

It's a good idea to list all the relatives, former employers, friends from school, people at church, and family friends you know who may have connections. Send them notes or call them on the phone to tell them you are looking for a position. Ask if they know of anything that's available.

Build good relationships with the people you meet at work. Know everyone your boss works with because he has worked hard to arrange his own network. If you go into the same business, you will already have a small personal network of your own.

It's a good idea to start now keeping a list of the names, addresses, and phone numbers of your friends and acquaintances. Each name may be a good contact for finding a job. Each Christmas send them all a Christmas card. Over the years you will find that when you need a position, or their children need work, you will be able to help each other. This mutual helping is called *networking*.

I maintain a list of approximately 1000 men and women I consider lifelong friends and acquaintances, and I update it once a month or so. As a result of having this list handy, I can find almost anything I want or need with two or three phone calls.

The first people I think of when I need a product or service are my friends. If I need a new copy machine, computer, or printer, I look at my list to see if anyone there sells what I need. That person could possibly help me get the best equipment for the dollars invested. And if I ever needed a new position, it wouldn't take many calls to find someone who knew of an opening.

The older you get, the more important it is to have friends whom you can call when you need help of some kind. And you can help the people in your network when *they* need something. Keep up your personal friends and acquaintances list. It will help you throughout your entire life.

KEY QUESTIONS
1. *Who are the people you would consider "lifelong friends" at this point?*
2. *How can you keep from losing track of these people as you grow older?*
3. *How have your parents kept track of their friends over the years?*

ACTION POINT
Make a list of your current friends' names, addresses, and phone numbers. Put the list in a place where you can keep it updated for the rest of your life.

SOCIAL

PRINCIPLES

For special gifts or services, make a game of saying "thank you" at least three different ways.

PRINCIPLE

67

"Of all the nerve! That person didn't even say thank you."
"See if I ever do anything for him again!"
"Well, the least you could do is say thank you!"

How many times have you heard comments like these made when someone did something very special, but did not receive appropriate appreciation? Whenever another person goes out of his or her way to do something for you, the effort should be acknowledged. Any time a person spends extra time helping you with something that will be beneficial, consider it a special gift and say thank you in special ways.

THE THANK-YOU GAME

One of the fun parts of life is learning to be creative when saying, "Thank you." You can express thanks verbally or by doing a small favor for the person (mow the lawn, bake cookies, help clean out the garage, etc.), but make a game of saying thank you in ways the person will remember.

For everything a person does for you, try to think of three or more ways to thank him or her. People are never offended by hearing "thank you" more than once. They may, however, be hurt or feel insulted if you don't say thanks at all, or if you do so in a way that is not meaningful to them.

WHEN YOU'RE THE OVERLOOKED PERSON

Can you remember a time when you did something very special for someone and it seemed they didn't even notice your effort? Perhaps you spent hours working on a project so it would be just perfect, but when you presented it, the person seemed distant. Did you feel resentment? Anger? Hurt? Did you make a silent resolution to withhold yourself from giving so freely to that person (and maybe others) again in the future?

Can you remember another time when you did something and the person appreciated it more than you ever expected? Not only did he say "thank you" personally, perhaps he wrote a note or even baked you some cookies!

Anytime someone does something for you, it's an opportunity to give lavish thanks and get the person excited about helping you again. Otherwise, such people are likely to be sorry they helped you at all.

KEY QUESTIONS

1. *Over the past weeks, who has gone "above and beyond the call of duty" to help you? Have you thanked those people in an appropriate way? If not, put this principle to use—today!*

2. *Think back over the last year. What are some things people did for you that you haven't yet thanked them for?*

3. *For the people you thought of above, what creative ways can you use to say thank you for the support, love, and care you received (even if you're a year late)?*

ACTION POINT

Say thank you in creative and meaningful ways to at least three people this week. Then make a lifelong habit of saying thank you in three different ways to people who help you out!

If you want to lose friends quickly, start bragging about yourself; if you want to make and keep friends, start bragging about others.

PRINCIPLE

68

If a friend tended to brag about herself and point out her superiority over you every time you got together, wouldn't that alienate you pretty quickly? Can you think of a much quicker way to lose friends than by bragging about yourself?

On the other hand, think of the people whose friendships you really enjoy. They probably do not brag about themselves. As a matter of fact, they are more likely to recognize *your* accomplishments and comment on how well you do, how good you look, and so forth.

FOCUSING ON OTHERS

When you have friends who make you feel good about yourself, you're happy to spend time with them and do things for them. You miss them when they're away. Your friends are the same way. They want to hear what they're doing *right*, not a list of petty criticisms.

An important skill to master is the art of complimenting people. Practice becoming "others centered." Keep asking yourself, "How can I creatively but genuinely compliment this person? How can I be more aware of what's going on in this person's world?"

HOW WILL THIS APPLY WHEN I'M ON MY OWN?

People who are self-centered as high school students tend to remain self-centered as they get older. The difference is, people understand that teenagers are not yet adults. Their selfish concerns can be blamed on youthful immaturity or insecurity. However, when you get to be an adult, people expect you to have outgrown the tendency to brag about yourself. The habit becomes just plain obnoxious!

Do you ever feel really uncomfortable, such as on the first day of school? You're concerned about looking right. You wonder if your friends will like your new hairstyle or your new clothes. You have a nervous feeling in the pit of your stomach.

The next time you experience that kind of feeling, remember that all of your friends probably feel exactly the same way. The Bible says, "Do to others what you would have them do to you" (Matthew 7:12, NIV—See Principle #96). The next time you're in an uncomfortable situation, focus your attention on the people around you. Notice *their* hairstyles, *their* clothes, *their* mannerisms, etc., and tell them what you like about them. You'll find that when you compliment others, they will tend to return the compliment to you!

KEY QUESTIONS

1. *If you brag about yourself often, why do you think you do it?*
2. *How do you feel about people who brag about themselves all the time?*
3. *What are three things you could always comment on about another person? (Hairstyle? Clothing? Jewelry? etc.)*

ACTION POINT

The next time you get together with a friend, spend the first several minutes complimenting that person. Focus your attention on your friend first, and yourself second. (Make sure you are sincere and that your comments sound natural.)

Concentrate on caring, not just conversations.

PRINCIPLE

69

It has happened to us all. You tell a friend about a very deep emotional crisis you're going through, and that person seems to ignore you and start talking about something completely different. You say you failed the test and feel terrible, but all he's concerned with is talking about how bad the teacher is—not how badly you feel. You say you just broke up with someone you dated for years, and she rattles on about her own bad dating experiences. Caring about someone requires more than just conversation. Two people may talk and talk and talk, but with no genuine concern shared between them.

CONCENTRATE ON CARING
Don't just talk to people; learn to care. Go beyond the person's words to his or her emotions.

My daughter Kimberly calls trivial, lightweight discussions "foo-foo" conversations. They center around things that don't really matter—gas mileage, the weather, or the latest basketball game. Learn to get to a deeper conversational level. Concentrate on really caring. Become involved in what your friends are feeling.

I recently had a conversation with an old friend of mine. While chatting over dinner, I was discussing the relationship I have with some of my friends. He asked, "Bobb, do you care for them?"

I said, "Sure! We're together all the time. We talk about everything. I'm with them a lot."

He asked again, "But do you care about them?"

I said, "Yeah, we talk a lot. We go places. We're friends."

Then he said, "Bobb, that's not what I asked you. What I am asking is . . . do you *care* for them?" Suddenly I began to understand what he really meant. I had been talking with my friends, but I hadn't been showing that I cared about them.

This was a hard lesson for me to learn. I didn't like seeing my own lack of concern. I've thought a lot about it since. That's the reason I included this principle in the book—to help you as you're developing relationships. Learn to really care about people and not just carry on conversations.

In life we may spend time with many people who disappear when we go through emotional letdowns. Adults are often guilty of this. Develop the quality of being "others centered" as a teenager, and you will have many deep, lasting friendships as an adult.

KEY QUESTIONS

1. *Who do you consider friends who don't really care about you?*
2. *Which of your friends do care about you personally?*
3. *How can you remind yourself to be a more caring person on a consistent basis?*

ACTION POINT

On a 3"x 5" card or a piece of paper, draw a square divided into 25 sections (five across and five down). Carry it with you. Each time someone shares a feeling or a concern with you, express your care and concern for the person. Later, when you're by yourself, put a check in one of the boxes. See how quickly you can get to 25 checks. This practice will help teach you to develop caring as a lifelong strength.

Never promise to keep a secret that will hurt someone.

PRINCIPLE

70

Being able to keep a secret is an important character quality. Revealing a secret is one of the worst betrayals. Being trusted to keep a secret is an honor, but it can also be a dangerous and possibly even deadly trap!

THE IMPORTANCE OF CONFIDENTIALITY

As a consultant, many people confide in me much as they would a pastor or an attorney. They expect to speak freely, knowing I will not repeat information, *whether or not they tell me it is confidential.* When no restriction is placed on our conversations, how do I know what information should be kept confidential? In my experience, confidential information breaks down into two basic categories:

(1) *Any information that is not public record*—For example, someone might tell you how much money their parents make, that their parents are getting a divorce, or that a friend's sister had an abortion. This kind of information should be kept confidential even if the person doesn't say, "Do you promise not to tell anyone?"

(2) *Insights into a person*—For example, a friend may share his greatest fears or concerns, or very private and possibly embarrassing (if made public) hopes and dreams. These kinds of insights should be kept confidential even if the person never asks you to do so.

It is an honor to be told something in confidence. Many people can't be trusted to keep a secret. Therefore, *when you accept the responsibility to keep a confidence, take it very seriously.* Never repeat

213

it to anyone. Even when you are no longer "closest friends" with that person, you still need to keep the confidences entrusted to you.

THE LIMITS OF CONFIDENTIALITY

As rewarding as it is to be asked to keep a confidence, you should never promise to keep a secret which will hurt someone.

Let's say a close friend comes to you and says, "Do you promise never to tell what I'm about to tell you?"

You say, "Of course I promise not to tell anyone."

Your friend asks again, "Are you sure? Do you really promise, sincerely, never to tell anyone—no matter what happens?"

You say, "Yes. I won't tell anyone. I absolutely promise."

Then your friend reveals he is planning to commit suicide!

Do you see the trap you've put yourself in? How will you feel if he goes through with it and you didn't say anything to anyone?

What if he says he's planning to kill someone? What if he's doing heavy drugs? Does your confidentiality help him or hurt him?

Such confidences may reveal that a friend is in deep trouble and needs help, and it would be in his best interests to contact his parents, his pastor, or school authorities. If you've promised not to say anything to anyone, do you see how difficult that could become? You will wish you had never promised to keep such a secret.

So use caution when you promise someone confidentiality. Simply add this small condition: "Sure, *as long as it isn't going to hurt you or someone else.*" Then if the person does tell you something that could be harmful, you have an "out."

You will occasionally find yourself in difficult positions, not knowing whether to speak up for the other person's safety or to keep silent for a while longer. But you'll learn from experience. Knowing when to speak up and when to keep silent is one more characteristic of maturity you'll need as you learn to live on your own.

KEY QUESTIONS

1. *How do you feel when someone asks you to keep a confidence?*
2. *How do you feel when you ask someone to keep a confidence and the person doesn't?*

3. How would you respond if someone asked you to keep a confidence, and then told you he was planning to harm himself in some way?

ACTION POINT

If you've already made a promise to keep a secret that could be harmful to someone, go to the person you promised and say, "You're going to have to let me out of this commitment. I didn't know someone was going to be hurt. Before I tell your parents (or the school), I needed to tell you."

PRINCIPLE

71

The best way to make a good friend is to be a good friend.

There isn't a person alive who doesn't want friends. But friendship is one of those things some people don't know how to create. They just don't seem to know how to make friends.

THE SECRET OF FRIENDSHIP

There are many ways to make friends. Some people "buy" them by paying for everything at the restaurant or movies. Others make friends through intimidation—by bullying weaker people into some kind of artificial relationship. Others act weak and rely on the pity of others. But of all the ways to get someone to be your friend, the best way is to be a good friend yourself.

What is a good friend? A good friend appreciates your company, likes to talk to you, listen to your advice, keeps confidences, protects your reputation, cares when you're depressed, gives you gifts, speaks well of you to other people, and much more.

You should make a list of all the things you feel are important in a good friendship. What are all the things you would like a good friend to be to you? Those are the very things you should do for the people you want to be your good friends.

BE A GOOD FRIEND

Once you make your list, consider which people you would like as friends. Begin doing the things on your list for the people you have in mind, and see if new friendships don't develop.

When it comes to friendships, adults have many of the same insecurities that children and teenagers do. After you're married, the question changes from, "Will I have a date for the party?" to, "Will I even be invited to the party?"

Other adult concerns are, "Will I be popular at the office?" "Will I be selected for the presidency or vice presidency?" "Will the people on my team follow my leadership only because of my title, or because they like me and want to work with me?" The situations may change, but the questions remain much the same.

Many adults wait for other people to be friendly before they allow themselves to be friendly in return. They respond to other people's friendship rather than initiating friendships of their own. It is far better to be a friend first, and then look for friendship in return.

KEY QUESTIONS

1. *Who are the five people you would most like to be friends with at this point in your life? Why?*
2. *How can you go out of your way to be friendly toward these people? How would you want them to go out of their way to be friendly to you if your situations were reversed?*
3. *Is there anything you're doing that may give people the impression you're unfriendly? (For example, sometimes a shy person can be accused of acting "stuck up.")*

ACTION POINT

Within the next seven days, decide on one person you would enjoy having as a friend. Go out of your way to do three things for that person as a gesture of friendship.

Caution: Be careful not to fall into the "Who's your best friend?" trap. By definition, a person can have only one best friend. Yet you can be a best friend to many people! Rather than speaking of a particular person as your "best friend," use the phrase, "One of my best friends." That way, no one ends up feeling left out.

PRINCIPLE

72

You can feel lonely in a crowd. You can also be all alone and not feel lonely.

Loneliness is one of life's most painful feelings. Most people have experienced the depression of feeling alone and uncared for. It's one of the areas you need to learn to deal with early in life because you will face occasional periods of loneliness throughout your lifetime.

LONELY IN A CROWD

Remember the last time you were in a group of people where everyone seemed to know each other, but no one knew you? You can be in a crowded room and still feel all alone. You can even be in a room filled with friends and feel lonely! Loneliness has little to do with how many people you're with at the time.

Loneliness strikes in many ways. There is *social* loneliness, which pertains to relationships with others. There is *financial* loneliness, where you may be under monetary pressures no one else knows about. There is *spiritual* loneliness, where you can be with a group of non-Christians yet feel lonely because you have no spiritual friendship. There is *professional* loneliness, where you are with people who do not understand your business.

ALONE AND NOT LONELY

As long as you remember you have family, friends, and people who love you, you're not as likely to feel lonely. Whenever you begin to feel lonely, make a list of such people. Even if they are far away, you'll feel a lot less lonely—even if you're still alone.

We should also remember that God is always with us. Ultimately, we are never truly alone. Jesus reminds us, "Surely I am with you always, to the very end of the age" (Matthew 28:20b, NIV). This promise helps eliminate some of the lonely feelings we have when we are isolated from friends or feel lonely in a crowd.

HOW WILL THIS APPLY WHEN I'M ON MY OWN?
Dealing with loneliness is a big part of growing up. As the old high school group splits up to go to college, get married, start jobs, and so forth, you'll have to cope with frequent aloneness. It's not uncommon for me to be alone while the kids are at school, when I'm on a business trip, or while Cheryl is visiting friends. People who don't learn to deal with loneliness can have miserable lives as adults.

Make the most of your relationships. Learn to depend on God when no one else is around. Master this while you're young and you'll never have to feel long periods of loneliness as an adult.

KEY QUESTIONS
1. *Who are the family members and friends you can always count on? Who can you depend on to be there through the good times as well as the bad?*
2. *Who can count on you to be there through the bad times?*
3. *What do you do when you feel lonely?*

ACTION POINT
Make a list of all your friends and acquaintances—the people you know and whom you want to keep as friends in the future. Then the next time you begin to feel lonely, get this list out and review it carefully. You may want to call one or two of the people. It will probably reduce your feeling of loneliness by at least 50 percent.

**Make a lifelong game of
remembering names!
People appreciate it.**

Have you ever experienced the awful embarrassment of forgetting a person's name? Occasionally we all do. But if we keep telling ourselves we're no good at remembering names, we won't be! You can and will improve with practice, so make a lifelong hobby of remembering names. See how many names you can actually remember over a lifetime.

NAME THAT PERSON

It is said that Napoleon Bonaparte knew 25,000 people by name. He was obviously an exceptional human being. He led his country to major military victories at the age of 28. He wrote laws in France which are still enforced today—hundreds of years later! He always had the loyalty of his troops behind him.

One reason Napoleon had such loyal followers was because he remembered their names! Doesn't it make you feel good when you meet someone once and he remembers your name the next time you see each other? And don't you feel lousy when someone keeps forgetting your name?

The average person probably knows 100 to 200 people by name, but we have the mental capacity to remember thousands of names! Practice remembering a person's first and last name. Associate the name with something about the person, but keep your facts straight.

Don't be like the man my father-in-law (Joe Kimbel) told me about. It seems this guy could never remember names. It was a real problem since he was a salesman who needed to recall the names of all the people he had met.

Finally he decided to see a psychologist for help. The doctor told him, "It's easy to remember names if you do it by association. For example, give me a name you find difficult to remember."

The man said, "Well, there is one person I have trouble remembering—the lady who runs the boardinghouse where I stay. She cooks all the meals, and it's very embarrassing when I bring a friend to dinner and can't even remember her name!

The doctor asked, "What *is* her name?

The man said, "Mrs. Hummock."

"Oh, that's an easy one," the doctor said. "Since she cooks meals for you, you can think, 'Mrs. Hummock feeds my stomach!' "

"Great!" said the man. "Now I'll remember her name for sure!"

A couple of weeks later, the man brought a friend home for dinner. As usual, his mind went blank during the introductions. Then he remembered what the doctor told him. He looked up confidently and said, "John, I'd like you to meet Mrs. Kelly."

THE TIME FACTOR

Just as you appreciate having your name remembered, so does everyone else. In one sense, the longer between meetings, the more impressive it is when you remember. If you go to your tenth high school reunion and people remember your name, that's pretty impressive. But if you go back to your twentieth reunion and they still remember your name, that's a whole other memory level.

Some people are very precise about the way their name should be pronounced. Be extra cautious to say their names the way *they* do. For example, I have a friend with a foreign name. He has told me of being offended by people in his organization who haven't yet learned to pronounce his name properly. As you learn names, be sure to get the pronunciation correct as well.

HOW WILL THIS APPLY WHEN I'M ON MY OWN?

Remembering names is important for social reasons and for the development of friendships over the years. But in adulthood, names take on an additional meaning. When people remember your name, they are more likely to do business with you. The same is true if you remember their names. What if you have a major client whose name you can never remember? He or she isn't likely to give you business for long. So make a hobby of remembering names. It will help you throughout your entire lifetime.

KEY QUESTIONS
1. *How many names do you know? (Think of a category—teachers, students, friends, relatives, etc.—and see how many names come to mind.)*
2. *How can you improve your ability to remember names?*
3. *How many new names have you learned during the past week? The past month?*

ACTION POINT
Make a list of all the friends and acquaintances you've made during your lifetime. If you can't think of both names, do some research and try to make the list complete. Keep adding people as they come to mind, and then update the list every month or so.

(Note: I personally keep a list called, "Lifelong Friends and Acquaintances." I record the names as, "Smith, Sam/Sally." I currently have 525 couples listed plus about another 50 or so single adults. Today I could probably recall about 1200 people by name. It may not seem like very many compared to Napoleon, but I'm still working on it!)

What you believe about people in general influences your behavior and attitudes toward individuals. You should assume that people: (1) do what makes sense to them; (2) don't want to fail; (3) want to make a difference; (4) want to grow; and (5) need to be encouraged.

PRINCIPLE

74

What you believe to be true about people in general shapes the way you treat everyone. If you believe people are basically lazy, you'll tend to become irritated and impatient when they don't do what you think they should. On the other hand, if you assume no one wants to fail, you'll tend to be patient, understanding, and helpful.

PEOPLE DO WHAT MAKES SENSE TO THEM

A professor I had at Michigan State University told the story of a high school freshman he once encountered. The boy had always been a model student. He had a slight build, and was certainly not athletic. In fact, he was what some people would call a "wimp."

One day during study hall, this model, straight-A student stood up and began stabbing a fellow student with a knife. His victim was a lineman on the football team who outweighed him by a hundred pounds, and could have easily "beaten him to a pulp" in seconds.

It took a couple of minutes for the shocked study hall monitor and a few other students to stop the boy from stabbing the football player. The injured boy was rushed to the hospital while the "model student" was taken to the principal's office. The school counselor (my professor) was called in to examine this extremely bizarre behavior. What would cause a person to go off the deep end like this?

My professor was a man who truly believed people do what makes sense to them. He asked the boy, "Why did you stab the football player?"

The boy responded, "For the last three days after school, he has cornered me in the alley on the way home. He hit me in the stomach, kicked me in the legs, and hurt me in ways you can't see when I have my clothes on. Last night he told me that tonight he was going to kill me on the way home, and I believed him. I knew there was no possible way I could beat him up, or even survive in the alley. I bought a knife and tried to kill him in study hall, before he could kill me."

Given the boy's thoughts, his behavior did not seem nearly so bizarre. His response is not to be recommended, but it does show that people do what makes sense to them!

Whenever people do something that seems off the wall, don't judge their actions until you can see the situation from their perspective. Their actions will probably then make sense.

PEOPLE DON'T WANT TO FAIL

Sometimes we see people on welfare or students getting D's, and we assume they don't care. We figure they simply don't care if they fail. But no one ever *wants* to fail. They just don't know how to win!

Think back to failures you've had in the past. Perhaps you failed a test or embarrassed yourself in public. How many of those failures were deliberate? My guess is, not a single one! You didn't want to fail, but you didn't know how to win. When you see a friend struggling or failing at something, why not see if you can help? Try to find a way to help the other person win. (See Principle #7.)

PEOPLE WANT TO MAKE A DIFFERENCE

One of the most penetrating things I learned during my five and a half years at World Vision International took place while I was business manager for the Korean Children's Choir. We were traveling, scheduled to do 97 concerts in 97 days! I decided if I was going to be away from my family for months on the road, I would learn something from every person I met. So I began to ask everyone the same question, "Why do you do what you do?"

I probably asked 150 to 200 people that question. I asked bus drivers, auditorium managers, promoters, ushers, school principals, businessmen, homemakers, teenagers—everyone I met! Nine times out of ten people would tell me, "I just want to make a difference. I want to leave this world a better place because I've been here."

People want to make a difference. You do. I do. One of the most basic things you can discover about a person is what difference he or she is trying to make, and then how you can help.

PEOPLE WANT TO GROW

Centuries ago, inside the pyramids of Egypt, people buried seeds with the Pharaohs. Those seeds have been dormant for over 2,000 years. Yet I understand if you plant and water one of those seeds, it will actually begin to grow. Amazing!

It always fascinates me to see a plant sprouting up through the crack in a sidewalk. Imagine a seed buried beneath cement finding its way to the surface. People are like seeds. Every single person wants to grow—to become stronger tomorrow than today.

As I write this paragraph, it happens to be New Year's Day. Around the world people are making resolutions to stay on a diet, to be more disciplined in study habits, etc. There are a thousand things we want to do to become better people during this new year!

Some people seem to think they'll never grow again as long as they live. But I see them as seeds in the pyramids. All they need is a little water and soil to begin to grow.

What is the "soil and water" that causes a person to grow? From my experience, "soil" is an environment of acceptance and "water" is encouragement. No matter how little concern a person shows toward growing, don't give up. If you begin to nurture such people with acceptance and encouragement, they *will* begin to blossom!

PEOPLE NEED TO BE ENCOURAGED

I have consulted with some of the country's finest leaders and their staffs. One thing I've found to be true of every single person is the need for encouragement. Everyone needs to believe tomorrow can be better than today, and that they can make a difference. A high percentage of people who quit jobs do so because they feel the boss doesn't care about their future on the job or their individual growth.

225

Many adults feel their spouses don't care about them, so they get a divorce. Many teenagers are discouraged with the relationships they have with their parents, and some end up running away from home due to lack of encouragement.

YOU CAN NEVER TELL . . .

C. S. Lewis was a great English writer who wrote *The Chronicles of Narnia* Series, *Mere Christianity*, and a variety of other classic Christian works. One day a friend saw Lewis treat a bum with great consideration and kindness. Surprised, the friend said, "I've watched you with both kings and paupers. You treat them the same! How are you able to do this?"

C. S. Lewis' response was simply this: "The dullest and most uninteresting person you can talk to may one day be a creature which, if you saw it now, you would be strongly tempted to worship, or else a horror and a corruption such as you now meet, if at all, only in a nightmare."

Whenever you make assumptions about people, try to see them as God sees them, with all their potential and strengths. Offer them hope and encouragement in all your dealings with them. And perhaps you will be fortunate enough for them to do you the same honor.

KEY QUESTIONS

1. *What assumptions do you make about people in general?*
2. *Do you agree with the five assumptions I've listed about people? If not, why not?*
3. *What assumptions do you think other people make about you?*

ACTION POINT

Make a list of the assumptions you make about other people, and discuss your list with your parents. Ask them to draw your attention to times in the future when you make improper assumptions about others.

Also try to think of one situation from your own life for each of the five assumptions.

When you are proud and stuck-up, everyone is happy when you fail. When you are humble and serving, everyone is happy when you succeed.

PRINCIPLE

75

Probably every person beyond the age of 2 1/2 has experienced the feeling of dislike toward a person who is "stuck-up." Most people outgrow their superior attitudes, but others struggle with them throughout their lifetimes.

When I was a kid, my friends (and I) used to tell certain people, "Don't get caught in the rain or you'll drown!" (Our observation was that the person's nose was so high in the air that rain would fall in and drown him!)

We all have ways of trying to cope with arrogant people, though none of them seem to work for long. Sooner or later most of us are happy to see arrogant people fail.

WHEN ARE OTHERS HAPPY FOR YOU?

Have you ever hoped a certain person wouldn't make cheerleader, get on the team, or be elected class president? You wanted to see the person fail because of his or her bragging and proud attitude.

If you act like you're the center of the universe and the world revolves around you, other people will see you as arrogant and stuck-up. They will cheer when you stumble and fall.

But when you're humble and serve others, everyone is happy when you succeed. We all know people who always seem to put others first. They go out of their way to help other people. When helpful and friendly people succeed, we are pleased for them and applaud their good fortune.

You may be tempted to think that when you become an adult you will outgrow childish ways of relating to proud people. But let me warn you—adults are as childish as second graders when it comes to being happy when proud people fail. And they are just as excited when they see humble, serving people succeed.

KEY QUESTIONS

1. *Who are the three most proud and stuck-up people you know? How do you feel about them—truthfully?*
2. *Who are the three most humble, serving people you know? How do you feel about them?*
3. *How can you become more humble and serving, rather than proud and stuck-up?*

ACTION POINT

Think of three things you can do to be a more serving person in regard to your parents, brothers, sisters, classmates, etc. Work on improving your willingness to humbly serve the people you know. When you find yourself succeeding, you'll find these people are happy for you!

If you know how to ask good questions and listen, you will never run out of great conversations.

PRINCIPLE

76

One of the most awkward situations in life is to be with someone and not know what to say. The uncomfortable silence between you just kind of hangs in the air. But if you learn to ask great questions and listen, you'll never run out of stimulating conversations.

ASK . . . AND LISTEN

Most people really want to talk. They have lots of things to say. What they need is a listener who cares enough to ask a few questions.

Just taking the time to listen to a person opens tremendous channels of communication. Most people simply don't take time to listen because our lives go by at such a hectic pace these days!

I've made a hobby of collecting questions on nearly every topic you could imagine. Let me share just a few of my favorites with you.

- If a genie granted you three wishes, what would they be?
- If you could talk with only one person in the world today, with whom would you want to talk? What would you discuss? Why would that be important to you?
- If God said you could do anything, anywhere, at any time, and you knew you couldn't fail, what would you do and why?
- If you were to go on a dream date, what would it be like?
- If someone gave you a million dollars but you had to spend it within three days, what would you do with it and why?

If you create about 20 or 30 questions like these and keep them in the back of your mind, you can fill several hours without running out of conversation. Take any of the questions you want from my list and add your own. Start with a list of about ten questions to memorize and add to it as you think of more. You'll never run out of something to say!

HOW WILL THIS APPLY WHEN I'M ON MY OWN?

You'll soon be expected to meet new people, get acquainted at parties, converse with clients, and do a variety of tasks requiring communication skills. You'll need to carry on conversations as well as listen to others. When you have a few good questions in mind, it doesn't take long to get a conversation started. And once it's started, you'll find that people are eager to give their perspectives on many different topics.

KEY QUESTIONS

1. *What are the five best questions you've ever been asked?*
2. *What kind of questions do you most enjoy being asked?*
3. *What kind of questions do you want to avoid at all costs?*

ACTION POINT

Make a list of ten questions to have available (and possibly memorize) for when you meet new people.

Note: A series of questions can also be helpful for making any major decision. In the appendix of this book you will find 30 questions to ask before making a major decision and 30 more to help think through a career decision. I hope these thoughts will help you make wise decisions and generate a lot of brilliant, breakthrough ideas!

Make asking and collecting questions a lifelong hobby.

PRINCIPLE

77

In addition to learning to ask questions to generate conversations (Principle #76), questions are also essential for gathering and clarifying information. None of us could get along in life without asking questions to help us solve problems and make decisions.

ASK QUESTIONS
We tend to ask a lot of questions when we are young. "Why this?" "Why that?" "Why not?" "How come?" As a result, we learn more at a faster rate than at any other time. But most parents become so tired of answering questions they begin saying, "Just because!" or, "Stop asking so many questions!" (Many of us did just that!) However, it's now time to revive the art of asking questions!

COLLECT QUESTIONS
If asking good questions is the key to solving problems, making decisions, and carrying on conversations, doesn't it make sense to collect some of the best ones? Some time ago I decided to make a hobby of asking questions. I now have a collection of probably 400 or 500 questions I can ask anyone, at any time. When I run into problems, decisions, or conversations, I use questions from my list.

A LIFELONG HOBBY
Collecting questions has been extremely helpful to me. I strongly recommend that you make collecting questions a lifelong hobby!

You may want to get a three-ring notebook with alphabetic tabs to record all the thoughts or questions that go running through your head. Some of the notebook categories could be:

- Ideas
- Plans
- Thoughts
- Lists of things to buy someday
- Things I want in a husband or wife
- Miscellaneous questions

This notebook can last your entire lifetime and be passed on to your children.

As a teenager, asking questions is critical. How would you ever get a date if you didn't ask for one? As you move into adulthood, one of the keys to maturity is being able to ask the right questions at the right time.

You want to carry on conversations that are meaningful, not just make "small talk." The older you become, the more valuable is your ability to ask the right questions. The right questions will help you in every situation, from getting the job you want to choosing the right mate. Therefore, make a hobby of asking questions, and you'll be ready for any circumstance that comes your way.

THE KINGDOM OF ASKEY

Journey with me into an imaginary land known as the Kingdom of Askey. In Askey everyone has a personal lockbox with valuable possessions in it—family heirlooms, jewels, patented formulas, secret ideas, notes about hopes and dreams, and other treasures. Unfortunately, many of the people have lost the keys to their lockboxes, and most of the kingdom's riches are locked away where no one can use them.

A poor boy began to collect every key he could find. Soon he had collected over a hundred keys of assorted shapes and sizes. One day he learned that a friend was among the people who had lost their keys.

The boy patiently began to test the lock on his friend's lockbox with one key after another. When he tried the 48th key, *bingo*, the box opened! Soon the boy was asked to help other people try to open their boxes. He discovered that some of his keys opened many boxes . . . some none . . . and others only a single box. But there were still many, many boxes that he couldn't open.

It occurred to him that he could make some brand-new keys in shapes he didn't yet have. Perhaps he could eventually unlock even the toughest of locks and free all the treasures of the kingdom.

He began to read everything he could about key making. He shared his thoughts with master key makers from other kingdoms. He experimented constantly. And with perseverance, he was able to unlock every single treasure box in the Kingdom of Askey.

Thus the parable of key making . . . and asking.

You will have many opportunities to "unlock" problems and receive valuable information. May you learn to create the right questions (keys) that will allow you to discover everything you need to know.

KEY QUESTIONS
1. *What are some topics you would like to know more about?*
2. *What are some questions you can ask to find out more about each of the topics you listed?*
3. *Who can best answer each of your questions?*

ACTION POINT
Make a list of the best questions you ever asked someone, or the ones you have been asked. You may begin with three questions, or thirty. But start your questions list today and add to it as you think of new ones.

 **By yourself you are alone, but with a friend you're a team of two.**

Most people enjoy being part of a team. We enjoy the camaraderie, the team spirit, and the sense of belonging. A team can usually accomplish far more than any individual can.

THE SINGLE-HANDED APPROACH
Many times in life we face situations all alone. But when we're alone, we tend to get discouraged. We sometimes lose perspective. We are limited by the amount of time and energy we can put into the project.

If you don't have someone else helping you reach your goals, you'll feel alone. If you aren't helping someone else reach their goals, you both may suffer from feelings of isolation and loneliness. (See Principle #72.)

THE TEAM APPROACH
You don't need fifty people working with you on a project to feel like you're a team. Just two people can compose a team, and a lot can be accomplished by a team of two! Whenever you're asked to do something, see if you can do it with a friend and it will seem to go better. Any project will go faster if you get just one other person to help—and it will be a whole lot more fun!

Whenever you're given something to do, ask yourself, "Which two or three people could help me with this project so that together we can accomplish more than I can alone?"

HOW WILL THIS APPLY WHEN I'M ON MY OWN?

One of the main reasons people get promoted in careers is because of their ability to form and lead teams of people. Any executive who can't work with a team finds his or her promotability is limited. The production of any one person can hardly stand up to that of a good team.

Get good at being part of a team. You can be a strong player on a team where someone else is in charge. Also try your hand at leading a team occasionally. You be the captain. But whether you're the leader or just one of the members, being part of a team is a fun experience. And don't ever forget—it just takes one other person to form a team.

KEY QUESTIONS

1. *What are you trying to do alone that you could do better with a team?*
2. *What people would you most enjoy having on your team?*
3. *Who are some people you would like to join forces with to help them reach their goals?*

ACTION POINT

Identify one thing you are trying to do alone. If you had one or two people helping you, would it go faster and be a lot more fun? Form a team where you're the captain and go to work on the task you have named.

PRINCIPLE

79

If you can't trust everything a person says, you can't trust anything he or she says.

How many times have you heard someone tell a "little white lie"? Does it make you wonder how much you can trust that person with anything else? Sometimes you may tend to think that even though he lies to parents and other friends, he'd never lie to *you*. But what makes you any different? Why would he lie to everyone else and not you? Eventually your trust in the person is likely to fade. Whether white lies, black lies, small lies, or big lies, *all* lies are lies!

THE PRICE OF DISHONESTY

It is an unusual person who can be completely truthful and loving at the same time. Our goal should be to always tell the truth—even if it is difficult for the other person to hear it—yet love the person so much that he or she accepts our comments anyway.

When a person asks how you like an outfit that you don't care for, what do you say? You don't have to say, "I love it!" when you think it's terrible. There are ways to phrase opinions without lying. You might say, "It's very different." Or you could be a little more direct and say, "Personally, I like your other styles better, but this look makes an interesting change."

You'll soon find that dishonesty (even an occasional "little white lie") leads to insecurity in a relationship. If you never know whether or not someone is telling you the truth, you can never fully trust that person. On the other hand, if the person *always* tells you the truth, you feel a real sense of security in the relationship.

236

If a person tells a "white lie," it doesn't mean he will never again say anything that's true. However, you can never be *sure* if what he says from then on is the truth. If you have a friend who is capable of lying, you can't have *complete* trust in what he or she says.

Honesty is one of the most basic foundations of the Christian faith and of all society. A society based on trust is a much stronger society. God gave us the Ten Commandments as basic guidelines to live by, and one of those ten is, "You must not lie" (Exodus 20:16, TLB). No matter what "size" or "color" of the lies, we need to eliminate them from our lives and our relationships.

KEY QUESTIONS

1. *What do you think about telling "white lies"?*
2. *Do you need to tell anyone, "I'm sorry. I told you a lie. Here's the real truth"?*
3. *How can you keep from telling any lies, or forming a habit pattern of telling "white lies"?*

ACTION POINT

Think of a person you've lied to in the last 30 days. Go to that person and "make it right." Tell the truth. Apologize for lying and promise not to do it again. And because you have sinned against God as well, ask Him to forgive you, too.

PRINCIPLE

80

"When visiting away from home,
eat what you're fed,
sleep where you're put,
and always say 'thank you!'"

EVIDA BIEHL

This principle is one my mother taught me when I was very young, and it has helped me a great deal in my adult life. Many people go to visit a friend and complain about the meals. They sometimes want to sleep in a place that causes extra work for the hostess. Then they say "good-bye" without even saying "thank you!"

EAT WHAT YOU'RE FED

When I was a teenager, I had very particular likes when it came to food. I usually preferred a hamburger, french fries, and a milk-shake. But I had no interest *whatsoever* in things like olives, oysters, cheeses, health foods, and certain vegetables.

Because of my mother's advice, I tried to take at least a small serving of whatever I was given—regardless of what it was. I learned to appreciate a wide variety of foods I would have otherwise missed. Today I eat almost anything I'm offered. I will have to admit there are still certain foods I haven't yet developed a taste for, but I plan to keep trying.

Trying new things when I stay in different homes has helped me grow up in terms of my taste buds as well as my social skills!

SLEEP WHERE YOU'RE PUT

One time our family was visiting relatives overnight. When it came time to go to bed, I asked if I could sleep in a place other than the one my aunt had assigned me. Wanting to be a gracious hostess, she made up a separate bed for me which required getting out clean sheets and doing a lot of extra work. Later my mother said, "Robert, don't ever ask a hostess if you can sleep anywhere other than where you're told. Do you see how much extra work she's going to?"

From that day to this, I've followed her advice. Occasionally I visit overnight with friends and sleep where they tell me. The one exception I make is if the home does not have a guest room and the host and hostess offer to have me sleep in their bedroom while they take the sofa. I much prefer the sofa to putting a couple out of their own room. But if they continue to insist that I sleep in their bed, I will agree. I don't want to press the point and embarrass them, or change their original plan.

ALWAYS SAY "THANK YOU"

You can hardly say "thank you" too many times! Based on experiences with friends of our children, I tend to want to give more and more to any young person who says "thank you." For those who don't, my natural tendency is to stop giving. Even though this may not seem very adult to you, most people feel this way.

My son J. had a friend named Cooper Williams. Cooper always thanked us for everything we ever gave him or did for him. After something like a week-long trip with our family, Cooper would stop by the house and give us a nice gift. Needless to say, Cooper Williams was always welcome to go on trips with our family. Obviously, he did not need to give us a gift to say "thank you." But it was a generous gesture which emphasized the fact that he was truly thankful.

HOW WILL THIS APPLY WHEN I'M ON MY OWN?

In some ways, elementary school kids are not expected to consistently say "thank you" for things you do for them. They are accustomed to being taken care of. In junior high, a little more responsibility is expected. Older teenagers are expected to eat what they're fed, sleep where they're put, and say "thank you." And any adult who does not abide by these basic rules of gracious manners is unforgivable! The better you can get at forming these habits, the better you'll do as you get out on your own!

KEY QUESTIONS

1. What lessons have you learned from staying with friends about foods you thought you didn't like?

2. What experiences have you had about sleeping where you're put?

3. What lessons have you learned about always saying "thank you" whenever visiting friends?

ACTION POINT

Discuss with your parents how they have felt about various friends you have had over. This will give you good insight into how other parents may feel about you!

We all learn most from friends, not enemies. If you want to convince a person of something, first become a real friend . . . then present your case.

PRINCIPLE

81

When all is said and done, when you shake everything out, the bottom line is that you trust your friends. You trust those who like you, but distrust those who don't like you. If you don't trust a person, you don't listen with an open ear no matter what he or she has to say.

So doesn't it make sense that before you can convince a person of something, you must first convince him you're a true friend? Abraham Lincoln said, "A drop of honey catches more flies than a gallon of gall." So it is with people.

BE A GENUINE FRIEND

Make a lifelong commitment of being a good friend to as many people as you possibly can. Don't make friends with people just to be able to convince them of things. Be genuine in your intentions. But you will find that once you become friends, convincing someone of your point is far easier.

In business this is called "networking." Smart leaders make friends with a lot of people and stay in touch with them. Over the years, they and their networks can help each other and learn from each other. You, too, should make friends whenever you can. (See Principle #66 for more good advice on networking.)

You will face many times when you will need to convince others to do certain things or to see things from your perspective. First be a true friend, and the convincing will come much more naturally.

241

KEY QUESTIONS

1. From whom do you learn the most?
2. Who do you feel learns the most from you, or is most open to your point of view?
3. Can you name a single person whom you dislike, yet continue to learn from?

ACTION POINT

Try an experiment. First think of something you would like to convince someone of. Then try to convince two people that your point of view is right. The first person should be a close friend. The second person should be someone who is a total stranger, someone you know but would not consider a friend, or even someone who doesn't like you at all.

See how each person responds to your attempt to convince him or her of something. I think you'll find this principle proves to be profoundly true in day-to-day experience!

When you influence a child, you influence a life. When you influence a father, you influence a family. When you influence a pastor, you influence a church. When you influence a leader, you influence all who look to him or her for leadership.

I clearly remember as a teenager the feeling of wanting to make a difference in life somehow, yet feeling like I had no power, position, or ability. Then one day my friend, Bill Bullard, drew a circle like a wagon wheel—something like this:

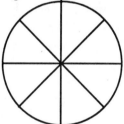

He pointed out that when you do anything to the hub of the wheel, you influence the whole wheel. That was the day I realized, "When you influence a child, you influence a life."

You constantly influence people whether you mean to or not. Any younger brothers, sisters, cousins, or other children who look up to you are influenced by the things you do. You help shape their lives whether or not you intend to.

Instead of seeing this as a heavy responsibility, look at it as an opportunity to make a significant difference. Right now the "little kid" who wants to hang around with you and be like you may be an annoying nuisance. But someday that very child may end up being a governor, senator, or possibly even the President of the United States!

Anything you can do to help younger people understand the principles you're learning (how to win, how to lead, how to succeed, how to get along in school, how to study, etc.) will influence them to be stronger adults. You have numerous opportunities to influence and make a major difference in someone's life.

THE POWER OF INFLUENCE

When you influence a person, you are influencing (indirectly) every person who ever looks to him or her for leadership. Suppose you influence a fourth grader not to do drugs, and that person grows up to become the governor of your state. Even as a teenager you will have influenced your entire state and every person in it!

You never know whom you're going to influence, or what influence that person will have on other people over the years. Look at the following example of the power of influencing others.

In 1858 a Sunday school teacher named Mr. Kimball led a Boston shoe clerk to Christ. The clerk, Dwight L. Moody, became an evangelist. In 1879 Moody awakened the evangelistic zeal in the heart of Frederick B. Meyer, pastor of a small church in England.

Meyer, preaching on an American college campus, brought to Christ a student named J. Wilbur Chapman. Chapman, who did YMCA work, employed a former baseball player, Billy Sunday, to do evangelism. Sunday held a revival in Charlotte, North Carolina. A group of local men were so enthusiastic afterward that they planned another campaign, bringing in a man named Mordecai Hamm to preach. In the revival, a young man named Billy Graham heard the Gospel and yielded his life to Christ. Each of these people who were influenced had a great influence on others in turn.

HOW WILL THIS APPLY WHEN I'M ON MY OWN?

Many adults feel successful, but not significant. They don't feel like they've made any real difference in the world. They think that life would certainly have gone on without them, and had they never existed, it wouldn't have made a bit of difference.

An example of this attitude is the classic Jimmy Stewart movie, *It's a Wonderful Life.* The main character thinks the world would have been better off if he had never even been born. The movie shows how an angel convinces him otherwise by demonstrating all the good that happened because he lived—as well as all the terrible things that would have occurred if he hadn't been there.

As you get older you will have many opportunities to influence future leaders. Anytime you are in a position to help people (perhaps by offering encouragement, teaching Sunday school, helping them develop a new skill, or praying for them), you make a difference.

You may recall people who influenced you when you were a child. Do you remember how much you looked up to them, and how every word they said meant something to you? Imagine what might have happened if the people who influenced you negatively had influenced you positively, or if those who influenced you positively had known how much it meant to you. That's the opportunity you have today to influence young kids who look to you in the same way you looked to your heroes.

You may think, *Well, I had heroes, but I don't think anyone looks at me that way.* Think again. The young kids looking up to you aren't going to say so. Just be aware that any younger child who knows you is looking to you for leadership, suggestions, a model, and ideas on how to grow up.

KEY QUESTIONS

1. *Who are three to five kids you would most like to influence?*
2. *How could you go out of your way to make them feel like they're okay? How can you let them know you want to see them do well?*
3. *What things have you learned from this book, your parents, or Sunday school that you think would be really helpful to teach them?*

ACTION POINT

List the three to five young kids you would most like to influence. Think about how you can help them become outstanding men and women of God. Decide today to do everything you can to provide a good model for those kids as they grow up.

PRINCIPLE

83

Needs which make you weep or pound the table wake up and unlock your creativity.

The needs you feel strongest about are most likely to inspire you to come up with a solution. Problems such as world hunger, abused children, and drug abuse need fresh ideas and thoughts. As you concentrate on such areas that you are most concerned with, new ideas will begin to come out of your mind. Often these are extremely creative ideas that someday will make a big difference.

NEEDS
Every original, creative idea I've ever had resulted from a need that made me want to weep or pound the table—where someone needed a solution to a problem and was sad or confused. When I saw those needs I began thinking, *What can I do? How can I solve this problem? How can I meet this need?* As a result, new ideas came to me that I'd never seen or considered before!

An often-repeated quote from the Book of Ecclesiastes is, "There is nothing new under the sun" (1:9b, NIV). As you read this quote in context, you can see that Solomon obviously didn't mean there would never be new inventions. Nor did he mean there is nothing a human can do which hasn't been thought of before. Computers and automobiles did not exist in Solomon's day. Every day people come up with things that have never existed before, and with new applications for existing information. You can still come up with original ideas and concepts, or solve problems which have stumped people for years and years!

WEEPING AND POUNDING THE TABLE
Unless you feel strongly about something, the likelihood of your following through on it is doubtful. But when you concentrate your energy on areas you do feel emotional about—problems that make you want to cry or hit something—you're in a much better position to develop and follow up new ideas.

It is important to realize you'll have hundreds of ideas in your lifetime, and you'll probably only follow through on a handful. But don't stop having good ideas just because you don't pursue all of them. In fact, you should have maybe 10 to 20 good ideas for every one that eventually becomes a serious goal.

UNLOCKING YOUR CREATIVITY
Once you identify a problem, your mind begins to think about it. You may "sleep on it," when suddenly an idea pops into your head! Focus on a problem like, "How can I help this older person?" Keep struggling with the problem for a while, ask God for new and creative ways to help, and I guarantee you'll begin to come up with new ideas and new possibilities.

George Washington Carver asked God to show him the secrets of a single little peanut. He then developed hundreds of formulas based on the peanut. With the money he earned from his discoveries, he started a whole university!

When you struggle with a problem that is of personal concern to you, over time you will develop many good ideas (and an occasional *great* idea) that will lead to a solution.

Everyone is creative, but not in the same way. Some people are *original*, and prefer to be given a problem and a blank sheet of paper. Some are *adaptive*, and like to be shown two or three examples from which they can create something even better. Some people use both methods almost equally.

As you continue to develop, you will better understand how your mind works. If you turn out to be an adaptive thinker, try to find some models, examples, or samples whenever you're given a problem. If you're original, then go off alone and try to figure out how to do something in a way you've never seen before.

247

While I was growing up, I don't recall anyone saying I was a creative person, and I didn't realize that everyone is creative. It finally occurred to me (at about age 23) that no one would tell me I was creative until I started being creative. So I began to come up with creative ideas for needs I could meet.

As a result, other people began to see me as creative. When asked to describe myself I'd say, "Well, I see myself as a creative person . . . " and pretty soon others began seeing me as creative, too.

IN CASE OF FIRE

Imagine you're on the sixth floor of a building when suddenly the fire alarm goes off! You see flames coming from the bottom of the building. You know you shouldn't use the elevators. There's no outside fire escape. You go to the stairway door, but feel intense heat and realize the flames are just on the other side.

It's my guess you'd think of a thousand different ways to get out of that building. You might think, *Could I call a helicopter? Could I jump onto an air bag? Could I get a fire engine here with one of those tall ladders?* Your mind would begin racing to figure out all the different ways to escape the fire! All of these different ways of getting out of the building are creative ideas. They are ideas or alternatives you wouldn't normally think of.

Whenever you're in a similar situation, your mind will begin coming up with creative alternatives. You *are* creative!

KEY QUESTIONS

1. *What three needs in the world would you do something about if you could?*
2. *What could you do about them?*
3. *Who could you influence to help you meet these needs?*

ACTION POINT

Think of the number one problem you would solve if you could. It doesn't have to be a life-threatening need. It could be as basic as collecting enough money to go on a vacation, buy something you want, feed a hungry family down the street, or help an older person who lives nearby. What need affects you deeply? What makes you weep or pound the table when you start thinking about it?

Sit down with a paper and pencil and see how many ideas you can come up with as possible solutions to meet that need. If you sit there for five or ten minutes and can't think of a single thing to do, get together with a few friends and do some brainstorming. Ask everyone to think of creative (original or adaptive) ideas for meeting that need.

"In a business decision, the wise man considers the effect on all of the people involved, not just the profit for himself."

DONALD E. SLOAT, PH.D.

PRIVATE PRACTICE PSYCHOLOGIST,

GRAND RAPIDS, MICHIGAN

As you grow up, you will soon realize that there are many people who do not have your best interests at heart. They are more than ready to take advantage of you, lie to you, and have you pay all the penalties while they get all the profits.

Of course, not every person on earth is crooked, dishonest, and out to get you. But it is unrealistic to expect that everyone wants the very best for you.

YOUR CHOICE

You can't always determine how other people will treat you. But you *can* choose how you want to treat other people. Remember the challenge of Matthew 7:12: "As you would have other people treat you, treat them in the same way." (See Principle #96.)

Whenever you are going to buy, sell, or invest in something, ask yourself, "Would I be happy if I were the other person? Am I treating others as fairly as I would like to be treated?" If you always follow the Golden Rule, you will find yourself with a very balanced perspective on managing money and conducting business.

I have found that the people who are most respected, appreciated, and trusted by others are those who treat people fairly—even when there is opportunity for taking advantage of someone. Such people resist the temptation even if the other person would never find out.

Living according to the Golden Rule not only earns people admiration, but also fosters trust in their future business dealings.

They develop positive reputations. Those who know them spread the word that they are good people to work with. And all of a sudden, they find new opportunities available to them that otherwise would go unnoticed.

This principle isn't limited to the area of money. It also applies to all kinds of decisions—even those your church youth group may be making. If a decision will benefit some at the expense of others, it's not a good choice.

One of the phrases you may have heard is, "To be a good deal, it has to be good for everyone." This is a true statement.

KNOWN BY REPUTATION

If you were to sit down and go over your list of lifelong friends and acquaintances, you would probably have a good idea as to whether or not each one could be trusted with money or be fair in a business situation. Each person has a reputation of being honest or dishonest.

Your reputation is important. Be consistently fair with other people. When others look at you, you want them to think, *This is an honest person! I can do business with him (or her)!* The stores, companies, businesses, and institutions that have a reputation for being honest, aboveboard, open, and trustworthy get more and more business. The ones that are seen as shady, unreliable, untrustworthy, and dishonest see their business begin to dry up.

KEY QUESTIONS

1. *Who is the most honest, dependable, trustworthy person you know? Would you enjoy being in a business relationship with him or her? How do you feel about this person?*

2. *Who is the shadiest character you know? Can you imagine getting into business with this person? How would it feel if other people saw you as shady, dishonest, and untrustworthy?*

3. *Have you ever been in a situation where you felt someone took advantage of you? How did that feel? Would you want that done to you again? Would you want the reputation of doing this to someone else?*

251

ACTION POINT

Go to the most honest person you know and ask about the benefits of maintaining honest relationships with people and caring about others. Listen to the person's wisdom. Note the benefits to be received by being a person who "considers the effect on all of the people involved, not just the profit for himself."

"The poor can act as our guides through the eye of the needle. When we help them, we find self-fulfillment and the wisdom that leads to the joys of the kingdom of God."

George Caywood—Executive Director

Union Rescue Mission, Los Angeles, California

"They're just lazy bums."
"They don't work, so I shouldn't have to feed them."
"Why don't they just go to work? I have to!"

You have probably heard statements like these many times in your life, and in many situations you might agree with them 100 percent. People who are healthy and strong *should* work, pay their own way, and take care of their own family's expenses.

However, there are people who are poor due to sickness, injury, lack of job opportunity, or crises (tornadoes, earthquakes, hurricanes, etc.). We need to do what we can to help poor, starving, people—especially when we have plenty.

WAYS TO HELP
This is not to say you need to take your entire savings account and give it to the poor. You need not stop eating in order to send all your food money to the poor. Yet, we should be generous in sharing with the less fortunate out of the money we do have.

Jim Burns, President of the National Institute of Youth Ministry in San Clemente, California, explained one day in a sermon how to determine if you are rich:

- Do you have more than one pair of shoes?
- Do you have more than one choice of what you will eat for each meal?

253

- Do you have access to your own transportation?
- Do you have more than one pair of underwear?

If you answered yes to three or more of these questions, then by world standards, you are a rich person. If we take the entire world and its entire inhabitants into account, we are actually a poor planet. Most people in North America are rich compared with those in many other countries, so we should learn to be concerned for those who don't have it as well as we do.

We can give things other than money. My son J. works in an area where there are many homeless people. Once he was working on a construction site when it started to rain, and was able to give one of the homeless men an extra tarp to provide shelter from the rain and cold.

If we only compare ourselves to our friends, it may be easy to feel like *we* are the poor when they have new cars, clothing, or stereos that we don't have. Therefore, we must try to keep a world perspective on what it means to be truly poor.

HOW WILL THIS APPLY WHEN I'M ON MY OWN?

As you get older, it will not suddenly get easier to share what you have with struggling strangers. Most adults do not find it easy to share their money with anyone. In some ways, the older you become, the higher the potential of developing a critical or cynical attitude.

Remember this principle: "When we help the poor, we find self-fulfillment and the wisdom that leads to the joys of the kingdom of God."

On a sobering note, the Bible, the absolute Word of God, warns: "He who shuts his ears to the cries of the poor will be ignored in his own time of need" (Proverbs 21:13, TLB). In our country, it may seem like we don't stand a chance of ever being truly poor. But all it would take is one tornado, one earthquake, one hurricane, or one fire to lose most of what we own and put us in the position of being poor and needing help from others.

KEY QUESTIONS

1. Who is the poorest person you know?

2. What poor people in the world make you feel sad? The hungry? The homeless? The victims of fire, earthquakes, etc.?

3. What could you do on your own to help the poor of the world?

ACTION POINT

It is not the purpose of this principle to overwhelm you with guilt for not giving your money or material goods to the poor. The goal is to help you feel the soul-filling joy which comes from sharing possessions with the poor. Therefore, I'd like to recommend that you take part of your savings and give it to a poor person. Buy something that the person needs or wants. Don't tell a living soul that you have done it, and experience the excitement, joy, and pleasure that come from giving—especially giving joyfully to the poor people of the world.

SPIRITUAL

PRINCIPLES

Before you trust a man or his message, study his life.

PRINCIPLE

86

Jesus. Hitler. Lenin. Mao. The apostle Paul.

All of these people had a lot of followers, though their teachings were quite different. How can you know whom to follow? Before you follow a man or woman, before you trust what he says, before you let him influence you, it's important for you to study his life.

Jesus lived a perfect, sinless life. His life was a reflection of what He taught. Other biblical figures and Christian leaders throughout history lived exemplary lives. They didn't just "talk the talk"; they also "walked the walk"!

Contrast these with some of our secular leaders who have had many wives (and mistresses), or were drug addicts or alcoholics. They may speak or write with great authority, but be cautious about following them. Their thoughts come from an immoral value system.

WHOM DO YOU TRUST?

My friend, Steve Arterburn, chairman and CEO of New Life Treatment Centers in Laguna Beach, California, has said, "Everyone knows how to play follow the leader. We're all following someone at some level. The question is, *whom* are we following?"

The most trustworthy person in all of human history is Jesus. He never led anyone into drug abuse, adultery, child abuse, or immorality of any kind. When you follow Jesus, you know you're following a trustworthy leader whose message reflected the way He lived His life.

Sometimes people publish things that are useful and true, but later seem like a mockery when the person does something in his own life that is inconsistent with what he wrote. A scandal in the author's life has ruined the success of many otherwise good books.

A SHAKY FOUNDATION

Dr. Bill Bright, founder and president of Campus Crusade for Christ, tells of a friend who visited with hotel entrepreneur, Conrad Hilton. Mr. Hilton carried the following information with him on a business card. It was titled, "Food for Thought."

In 1923, a very important meeting was held at the Edgewater Beach Hotel in Chicago. Attending this meeting were nine of the world's most successful financiers.

Those present were: the president of the largest independent steel company, the president of the largest utility company, the president of the largest gas company, the greatest wheat speculator, the president of the New York Stock Exchange, a member of the president's cabinet, the greatest "bear" on Wall Street, head of the world's greatest monopoly, and president of the Bank of International Settlements.

Certainly we must admit that here were gathered a group of the world's most successful men. At least, men who had found the secret of "making money."

Twenty-five years later let's see where these men are:

The president of the largest independent steel company, Charles Schwab, died bankrupt and lived on borrowed money for five years before his death. The president of the largest utility company, Samuel Insull, died a fugitive from justice and penniless in a foreign land. The president of the largest gas company, Howard Hopson, is now insane. The greatest wheat speculator, Arthur Cutten, died abroad, insolvent. The president of the New York Stock Exchange, Richard Whitnesy, was recently released from Sing Sing Penitentiary. The member of the president's cabinet, Albert Fall, was pardoned from prison so he could die at home. The greatest bear on Wall Street, Jesse Livermore, killed himself. So did the president of the Bank of International Settlements, Leon Fraser.

All of these men learned well the art of making money, but not one of them learned how to live.

I'm not suggesting you need to study the life of every author before you can recognize the rightness in what he or she has to say. But before you let an individual influence you with his value system, find out if he actually lives by that system. If someone gives you advice on marriage, but you discover that he has been married four times, you are not likely to trust him as much as a counselor who has been happily married for twenty years.

A DANGEROUS TRUST

You may remember hearing about the Reverend Jim Jones and the People's Temple. Jim Jones was a cult leader in San Francisco who moved several hundred of his followers to the jungles of Guiana. He exerted total control over them and gained their complete trust.

But Jones was an evil dictator. When the truth about him was about to be revealed to the world, he convinced his people to commit mass suicide by drinking a deadly mixture of Kool-Aid and poison.

Many of Jim Jones's followers had given him their entire fortunes. Had they studied his life, they would have found him to be shallow and immoral. They wouldn't have trusted his message. Don't make the same mistake. "Before you trust a man or his message, study his life."

One word of caution: Even if a person's life has measured up to your expectations, measure everything he says using the Bible as a standard. (See Principle #87.) Whenever someone—anyone—tells you something that disagrees with Scripture, trust the Bible.

KEY QUESTIONS

1. Which three people do you trust most?
2. Why do you trust them?
3. Whom don't you trust because of the way they conduct their lives?

ACTION POINT

Make a list of the three to five people you trust most. Beside each name, jot down a few notes to explain why you trust that person.

PRINCIPLE

87

God's Word, the Bible, is the world's only completely trustworthy measuring stick for truth. Without the Bible, there is no absolute standard for right or wrong.

What happens when I die?
Is there really a God, and if so, what is He like?
Does God care that my friends are getting abortions?
What's wrong with the "Look out for #1" philosophy?

Without an absolute standard of right and wrong and a trustworthy measuring stick for truth, answers to questions like these are only some person's opinion. It is extremely important to have a source of absolute truth. Without it, everything becomes just your opinion against someone else's. Discussions are limited to your own experiences compared to another person's. Perspective is also limited when you need to make major decisions.

TRUTH DOESN'T CHANGE

Many issues today seem clouded by one television commentator's views versus another's—or even one teacher's views versus another's. We can discuss our opinions with friends and family members, and ask our teachers or professors, yet still come to the wrong conclusion!

Decisions based on personal opinion, experience, and prejudice are likely to change with any new wave of popular opinion and put us in a total state of confusion. But we have available the Bible, the source of all truth—unchangeable truth.

Josh McDowell wrote a book entitled *Evidence That Demands a Verdict* (Campus Crusade). If you ever have doubts about the reliability of the Bible as the Word of God, study the evidence carefully before you decide that the Bible is simply another book. The following assumptions are an important foundation for your life:

(1) There is a God.

(2) He cared enough about us to give us the Bible.

(3) The Bible is the trustworthy basis of truth and the absolute standard for right and wrong.

As you keep these three assumptions firmly in your mind, you will have a solid foundation on which to build your life. It's like the song many of us learned in Sunday school about the foolish man who built his house on the sand. When the floods came, his house was washed away. But the wise man built his house on the rock, and it stood firm through the storm (Matthew 7:24-27). God's Word is our rock.

A TRUSTWORTHY MEASURING STICK FOR TRUTH

The world contains many elements of truth. Some truth is discovered through personal experience. There are laws of nature. There are even bits of truth tucked away in various philosophies and theologies that, as a whole, are untrue. But the only completely trustworthy measuring stick for truth is God's Word, the Bible.

AN ABSOLUTE STANDARD OF RIGHT AND WRONG

Think for a moment . . . how can you determine what is true from what is false without some kind of a measure? It's impossible! Without an absolute standard of some kind (never changing, always reliable), how can you decide whether something is right or wrong? You can't! Without the Bible, there is no consistent standard.

HOW WILL THIS APPLY WHEN I'M ON MY OWN?

When you move away from home, you will encounter many people with differing philosophies, theories, theologies, perspectives, and opinions. They will try to convince you they are right—and that what you've been taught all your life is wrong. That's when you will need a way to determine whether these different approaches to life are right or wrong.

This is especially true in college where you may encounter professors who do not share your views of truth. It's important to have the Bible as a standard, rather than just your own opinions. Quoting the Bible gives authority to the issue.

Because your beliefs will be challenged, it's important to know what you believe and why! Reading books like *Evidence That Demands a Verdict* will provide a wealth of solid facts. Brilliant scholars have spent years documenting the fact that the Bible can be trusted. Even though you may not know all the answers, you can still believe that the Bible is the only trustworthy, absolute standard for determining right and wrong.

Frankly, it doesn't matter a lot what my opinion is, or what your opinion is, or what some professor's opinion is. The real question is, "What does God Almighty, the creator of *everything*, have to say about what is right or wrong?"

KEY QUESTIONS

1. *Do you agree that there is a God?*
2. *Do you agree that the Bible is His Word to us?*
3. *Do you agree that the Bible is the only absolute standard of right and wrong?*

ACTION POINT

Discuss with your parent(s) your thinking on the three basic assumptions:

(1) There is a God.
(2) He cares enough about us to give us the Bible.
(3) The Bible is the trustworthy basis of truth and the absolute standard for right and wrong.

When God seems far away, focus on biblical answers that cannot be questioned rather than life's questions that cannot be answered.

Sometimes I feel overwhelmed by questions that seem to have no answers: "Why do some small children get cancer?" "How can I prove to my friends that God is real?" "Why do we have war?" "Why doesn't God do something about the starving people in Africa?" "What about the homeless?" The list goes on and on.

If I spend too long on these unanswerable questions, I begin to feel tension. But I've found that focusing on what I *do* know—rather than what I *don't* know—relieves a lot of internal pressure.

WHEN GOD SEEMS FAR AWAY

Sometimes I feel very close to God. But to be honest with you, there have been a lot more times when I've felt very distant. When I feel that way, I think of a bumper sticker I once saw. It read, "If you feel far from God, guess who moved?"

The reason most people try to keep God at a distance is the fear that if they get too close, He might ask them to stop doing something they don't want to stop. However, being close to God reduces anxiety, insecurity, and fear. It is wise to make a habit of staying as close to God as you possibly can.

ANSWERS THAT CANNOT BE QUESTIONED

Many things in Scripture are very, very clear. Don't kill. Don't steal. Don't take God's name in vain. These commandments, along with other principles and promises are spelled out specifically.

When God seems far away, focus on the things you know are absolutely clear in the Bible that apply to your life.

You may also want to focus on the positive things in your life: "I have a parent (or parents). I have a home. I have clothes to wear. I have a church to attend. I have friends." Focus on what you *do* have . . . not what you don't have.

Many things in life will never be clearly understood. That's why it's so important to first define the things we have, the things we know, and the things we believe. Then we develop a better perspective on answers we don't have yet as well as confidence that those answers will become clearer over time.

LIFE'S QUESTIONS

The Bible doesn't promise that all our questions will be answered in this life. "Now we see through a glass, darkly; but then face to face" (I Corinthians 13:12, KJV). When difficult questions start overwhelming you, recall some of God's promises and allow them to comfort and assure you. Begin putting together a list of the things you know are true so you don't lose track of what you *do* believe: "There is a God. He loves me so much, He was willing to die for me. I don't understand why this happened, but I can trust Him."

Remember that we won't have answers to some things until we get to heaven. In the meantime, never lose sight of the sure and certain things that make living such a wonderful privilege.

KEY QUESTIONS

1. *What are the things you believe to be true?*
2. *What are the positive things in your life?*
3. *Who are the three wisest people you know who can provide godly perspective on your questions?*

ACTION POINT

Make a list of all the things you truly believe. It may take five minutes or five hours. Then think about your list, discuss it with your parents, and be ready to pull it out the next time you confront one of those "unanswerable" questions.

"He is no fool who gives that which he cannot keep, to gain that which he cannot lose."

Jim Elliot

Missionary to the Auca Indians in Peru

PRINCIPLE

89

As a teenager, I remember being very concerned that God might call me to Africa as a missionary if I committed my life to Him. But in time I got to the point where that idea was all right with me. I realized I would rather have a relationship with God (no matter what He might ask of me) than to have no relationship with Him. I'd rather spend eternity in heaven (no matter what the cost now) than to be forever separated from God.

NO FOOL

"He is no fool," means the same as saying someone is really smart, clever, or wise. It means the person does the right thing. He or she makes the right choices.

You can easily distinguish between an immature and a mature person. An immature person wants rewards and good times immediately. A mature person is willing to give up those things today in order to have better things later. The immature person wants a car—any car—and he wants it now! The mature person is willing to wait an extra year to earn more money for a nicer car.

Some people get involved in drinking, drugs, casual sex, and so forth, because those things feel good *now*. They don't stop to think about the future consequences to their bodies or their lives. But a sign of maturity is the ability to postpone potentially harmful experiences at this point in order to achieve a more worthwhile and lasting satisfaction later.

WHAT YOU CANNOT KEEP

It may not be a pleasant thought, but we are all in the process of dying from the minute we're born. Looking ahead during your teenage years, approximately 70 years of life can seem like a long, long time. But in the scope of eternity, it's just a speck . . . about as long as a nanosecond!

We cannot "keep" our lives. When we forget this, we tend to make unwise choices concerning things that may bring temporary pleasure, but could ruin us later.

WHAT YOU CANNOT LOSE

Yet even though our lives are temporary and will eventually come to an end, a Christian's relationship with God is permanent and everlasting. We can count on spending eternity with God in heaven.

Heaven is one of a Christian's most motivating assurances. It is a place where there is no sickness, no sadness, no crying, no divorce, no drug overdoses, no drunkenness, no rejection, no embarrassment, no riots, and no boredom. Heaven will be perfect! God will be there to answer any questions we've ever had, wipe away all of our tears, and give us complete peace and security. Any sacrifice we make in this life is small compared to the wonder we will experience in heaven.

Jim Elliot lived—and died—by what he believed. As a young missionary in the jungles of South America, he was killed by the natives he had gone to help. Yet his life and death influenced the entire tribe to receive Christ and eternity in heaven as well.

THE SOONER THE BETTER

I remember feeling that my teenage years were intended for fun. I assumed when I got to be in my 20s, I wouldn't have as much fun, so it would be a good time to commit my life completely to Christ.

When I got in my 20s I thought, *Well, I'm in school now. It's still not a good time.* In my 30s I thought, *Things are going too well here. I have a house, a family, and responsibilities. If I give my life to Christ completely, He may ask me to take a different job or move somewhere.*

In my 40s I came up with more reasons to put off further commitment. Yet after I finally decided that God knew better than I what was best for me, I never regretted making the decision to give Him control of my life. (I just wish I had done it a lot sooner.)

In every phase of life you will find excuses not to trust Christ completely. If you realize this now, perhaps you won't make the mistake of wasting so much time!

A CHANGE FOR THE BETTER

Think of a baby, warm and cozy, in its mother's tummy. Imagine the baby can talk. After nine months, it's about to be born. Mama says, "Well, it's about time for me to introduce you to a big, beautiful, new world with its colors, lights, and music! When you grow up, you'll go on dates, have parties, shop for clothes, go to ballgames, listen to radios, and take summer vacations!"

But Baby says, "No, thanks. I'm warm in here. I'm comfortable. I'm happy. No one bothers me. I don't want to leave!"

Mom responds, "But you can learn to play baseball, eat ice-cream cones, go for walks in the woods, and roll in the leaves. It's much better out here than in there. Don't you want to do all these new things?"

Baby says, "No, thanks. I like it here just fine."

Think how shortsighted it would be for an unborn baby not to want to enter this bright, new world. Yet the new world is unknown while Mama's womb is familiar, and change is always a little frightening.

When God says to us, "It's about time for you to make a commitment to Me and prepare to go to heaven," we say, "No, God. I want to stay the way I am. It's so wonderful here. I know this world. I know my friends, my school, and my city. I know how to get a job here. I know how humans think, but not how angels think."

Then God says, "Well, yes, but in heaven there's no crying, no divorce, and no pain. You'll see your grandparents again and get to meet your great grandparents! You can get to know the apostles and disciples and all the wonderful people of history. You get to be with Me forever."

But you may still say, "No, I think I'm happier here."

Heaven will be so much greater than this earth has ever been. It will be fantastic. It's something to really look forward to.

You are certainly no fool if you give up something you cannot keep to gain something you cannot lose.

KEY QUESTIONS

1. *What would be the hardest thing God could ever ask you to give up? Would you rather have that thing, or the assurance of going to heaven?*
2. *How do you feel about dying someday?*
3. *What do you imagine heaven will be like? What do you most look forward to about going there?*

ACTION POINT

Make a list of all the wonderful things about heaven. If you're not aware of what heaven will be like, read all the Bible verses which tell about it. You may also want to read a book or two about heaven because it is going to be an incredible place!

Ultimately we do everything for one of two reasons: To serve ourselves, or to serve God.

PRINCIPLE

90

We all do things without thinking about why we do them. But some-day when you're just lying in the sun thinking about life in general, consider how many options you have, and why you do what you do. What's at the center of your universe? Is it you, or is it God?

SERVING OURSELVES

Everything ultimately boils down to the things you do to look good, feel good, or get a reward of some kind . . . or things you do to bring glory and honor to God. Even when you do things for other people, you tend to do them either for yourself or God. Do you help the older lady across the street so God will be praised, or so you get a "pat on the back" for being so helpful? Do you help needy people out of Christian love, or so you will feel good about yourself?

One of Satan's greatest tools is our self-centeredness. There is an appropriate sense in which you have to watch out for yourself, of course. You should use common sense about going into areas at night where people might rob, rape, or kill you. And you want to be aggressive at work and let your boss know you're doing a good job to get promotions. But if the only reason you do something is to get yourself ahead and not to help God in some way, then ultimately what you're doing is self-centered.

I'll never forget an experience I had in my early 20s. One day I realized that if a string stretched out for a thousand miles in either direction of me, I could not put one ear on the string and look at both ends of the string at once. It was a physical impossibility. In the same way, we cannot focus on God and money (or God and ourselves) at the same time. We must direct our attention to one end of the string or the other.

SERVING GOD

As a teenager I struggled not only with the idea of serving God, but also with the question of His very existence. I no longer have those doubts, but I remember wondering, "Is there really a God, or not?"

Many things helped me regain my deep belief and trust in God. One was the reality that since the time Jesus walked on our planet, millions of people smarter than I am have studied Scripture and concluded that God exists. Such a conclusion doesn't *prove* the existence of God, yet it was important for me to see that so many wise adults do believe in God! Also, the fact that the Scriptures have survived for thousands of years is another evidence of the existence of God.

If you struggle with similar questions, you may want to read Josh McDowell's book, *More Than a Carpenter* (Tyndale). God does exist and there is proof for it . . . much, much more than I ever dreamed when I was a teenager growing up.

HOW WILL THIS APPLY WHEN I'M ON MY OWN?

Adults can easily get caught up in the bigger house, bigger car, more money rat race. The desire for comfort leads to the accumulation of more and more things. We need to keep asking, "What am I doing that makes an *eternal* difference? Why am I doing what I'm doing?" Otherwise, when we get to the end of a selfish, self-centered life, we will feel no satisfaction and discover that we have stored up no treasure in heaven whatsoever. That's what we can expect when we try to please ourselves. It is much more fulfilling to determine to please God instead.

KEY QUESTIONS

1. *Ninety-five percent of the time, why do you do what you do? Is it to serve God or yourself?*

2. *What one thing could you do in the next three days to really serve God? (Perhaps no one else would even know about it.)*

3. *What could you do in your life at this point to make a commitment to serve God rather than yourself; to build His kingdom, not your own; to give God glory because you've lived?*

ACTION POINT

Think back to the last thing you did that you were extraordinarily proud of. You may have won a track meet, been captain of a team, won a debate, or been elected to class office. It could even be as simple as getting your group of friends to go with you to a concert. Then answer the question, "Why did I do that? Was it a self-centered reason, or was it a God-centered reason?"

PRINCIPLE

91

God's timing is perfect.

As a teenager, it felt like my timing was off on everything! But the older I got, the more I began to see that God's timing is perfect—even when it differs from mine!

God has a plan for the world and for each individual life. Nothing is outside of His control.

Dr. R. C. Sproul, says, "There's not a single maverick molecule anywhere in God's universe." Everything is under God's ultimate control, and His timing is perfect.

A DIFFERENT PERSPECTIVE

There will come a time when you'll look back on your life and see how beautifully the events fit together. Perhaps you'll realize if you had gone to camp the week before (like you had planned), you wouldn't have met the person who is now your best friend. Or if you had been accepted at the other school, you would have never met the person you married. You'll look back and see that God's timing has been perfect in your life—down to the week, down to the day, down to the minute!

One reason this is so critical is because you want to be able to be comfortable with who you are and where you are at this point in your life. You can continually worry that you should be doing more, doing better, or doing things differently. Or you can simply trust that God cares for you and is in control of your life.

PEACE OR PANIC?

Let me give you a personal example. A few years ago I was scheduled to go to Europe for a consultation with a large Christian organization. My son J. was going with me. He planned to ski in the German Alps while I lectured at the conference. We got to the airport in plenty of time to catch our international flight, so we decided to have one more fast food American hamburger before we left!

When we got to the restaurant, I said to my wife, Cheryl, "You've got the passports, right?"

She said, "No, you've got them."

I quickly looked through my things, and then panic set in. The passports weren't there.

We left the restaurant and checked everywhere we could think of. We rushed back to the ticket desk and asked if anyone had turned them in. No one had. We began to suppose that someone might have stolen them, because they can be sold on the black market.

What had begun as a leisurely hour before we caught a flight turned into a frantic hour of searching for two passports. We went to Visitors' Aid. We went to other ticket counters. We called the American Embassy to see if they could replace the passports in that amount of time. (The answer was no.)

I thought of the people coming from all over Europe to the conference. It was too late to alert them not to come. If we didn't meet this week, we wouldn't be able to reschedule for another year. All the materials had already been sent and it would be a major problem to recover them. And J. would miss out on skiing.

By this time we were running through airport corridors trying to find "Lost and Found." The pressure was on! Finally I just stopped and prayed, "God, I thank You that Your timing is perfect. If this is not the time for J. and me to be in Europe, I rest in that."

Five minutes later, we got a call from the Airport Police. They had found the passports! We rushed over to pick them up and got back to the airport just as passengers were beginning to board. Five minutes more, and we wouldn't have gone. One hour sooner and I wouldn't have learned the lesson. I wouldn't have been able to put my faith to the test. I was facing severe disappointment because it seemed that all my planning was going to be for nothing. But once I stopped focusing on myself and left it all up to God, I began to trust that His will would be done, and that it would be for the best. God's timing is always perfect.

KEY QUESTIONS

1. *What are three times in your life when God's timing has been perfect?*
2. *What can you learn from your parents about God's perfect timing?*
3. *What are some things you can do to keep from forgetting that God's timing is perfect (so you won't forget this principle when you need it)?*

ACTION POINT

Look back over your life and think of a time you came close to getting in with the wrong crowd or making a mistake of some kind. Think of how maybe one word, one person, or one day made the difference that prevented you from getting into trouble or making a very unwise decision.

"Giving to God and others is like the farmer planting seed. The more he plants, the greater his harvest."

RICH BUHLER—HOST

"TALK FROM THE HEART," KBRT, LOS ANGELES, CALIFORNIA

PRINCIPLE

92

Have you ever asked yourself, "How much money do I have to give to the church? I never have enough money for myself, let alone for giving some to others. Give money to the poor? I *am* 'the poor!'"

The topic of giving seems to be one typically reserved for pastors on Sunday morning, but the Bible says a great deal about it. The reason God says so much about giving is not that *He* needs what we give. Rather, giving is important because *we* need to give!

THE PROMISE OF GIVING

Have you ever had the experience of giving something to someone with no possibility of anyone ever finding out who gave it, how much was given, or that you were even involved? This anonymous giving is one of the most rewarding things a person can ever do, yet we rarely think of it as an option, let alone a biblical command.

The Bible not only talks about giving as a duty or commandment, but it also talks about the *promise* of giving. The one who gives with a cheerful heart will have his supply replenished in even greater amounts than he has given, whether in monetary terms or other benefits (II Corinthians 9:6-11).

This is where Rich Buhler's wisdom comes into focus. You may have heard people say, "You can't outgive God." This is exactly what Rich is talking about. The more you give to God and other people, the more you will have returned to you.

When God commands that we give to the poor, it is to benefit

277

us as well as the other person. Giving encourages us to go beyond selfish human nature and experience true joy. You may think, *What a joke! How could that possibly happen, that I could give to one person, and then, from totally different sources, I receive whatever I need?* I can't explain how God works in every instance; I just know that He promises: "Give, and it will be given to you" (Luke 6:38, NIV).

HOW WILL THIS APPLY WHEN I'M ON MY OWN?
It may surprise you to find that it doesn't become easier to give to others when you get older. The older you get, the more financial commitments you have to make. In some ways, giving becomes even more difficult. But remember: the more you give, the more God returns to you in different ways.

KEY QUESTIONS
1. *What percentage of your money or valuable things are you giving to God and other people at this point?*
2. *What percentage would you like to give?*
3. *What has been your experience with giving in the past? Have you experienced the joy of giving money that no one finds out about—"anonymous" giving?*

ACTION POINT
During the next 30 days, experiment with giving. Give something in a totally anonymous way to someone who is needy, and then see how quickly God returns the gift you've given, plus some. And don't forget to thank Him when He gives something back!

Assume God and people like you, and things will work out.

PRINCIPLE

93

We all know people who seem to be negative about everything! They automatically jump to the conclusion that no one likes them and nothing's going to work out right.

If you know someone in this category, here is a fascinating thought to share with the person: *Everything has at least a fifty-fifty chance of working out to the positive.* There's a fifty-fifty chance the stranger you meet today will become a best friend rather than an enemy. There's at least a fifty-fifty chance things will work out rather than fall apart. Some people waste a lot of time worrying about things that never happen.

ASSUME GOD AND PEOPLE LIKE YOU

The Bible promises, "For God so loved the world that he gave his one and only Son, that whoever believes in him shall not perish but have eternal life" (John 3:16, NIV). You don't have to *hope* God likes you . . . you can *know* it. Trust that God loves you because He gave His only Son for you.

As for people, most will end up liking you if you have any positive, pleasant attitudes at all. People tend to like other people. There is a better chance they will like you than not. So unless it's obvious they don't like you, assume they do!

It's much better to go through life wrongly assuming people like you than to wrongly assume they don't. I'd much rather be wrong believing people like me!

THINGS WILL WORK OUT

I had a relative who was convinced things would never work out. Every day of her life she assumed things would go badly. If a friend was late for a lunch, she became convinced he wasn't going to show up, that he didn't like her anymore, or that he had been in an accident. When many things in her life *did* work out, she had wasted too much time and energy being negative to appreciate them.

When you're working on a project with people, keep talking about how much progress you're all making. People sometimes get so caught up in running the race and reaching the end goals they can't see they've already run five miles of the marathon. It may seem they haven't made much progress at all.

Every time you see a person make progress, comment on it. "Hey, we got another two rows done." "If we keep this up, we'll be finished before we know it." "You sure have grown a lot." "It's easy to see you've lost weight. Your diet is working. Keep it up."

Making progress is encouraging, but having someone notice your progress is even better! If you don't see obvious progress, keep working at it. Keep alive the hope within yourself and within others that, in fact, "We're making progress!"

Imagine you have two friends in the room with you. One is always positive about the future. The other is always negative and complains about everything. Which one do you prefer to spend time with? Most people like to be with positive people and don't like to be with negative people. It's as simple as that!

KEY QUESTIONS

1. *Who is the most positive person you know?*
2. *Who is the most negative person you know?*
3. *Which person do you enjoy being with more . . . and why?*

ACTION POINT

Try an experiment: Make positive assumptions about everything for the next three hours! The minute you think negatively, start the clock again. Keep trying until you can be positive for at least three hours. See how it feels!

Your attractiveness is a combination of the outer you, the inner you, your dreams, and God's blessing.

I am often fascinated when I consider why I do or don't like a certain person. I know some people who are very handsome or beautiful, but I don't like their negative and critical characters. Others aren't especially attractive physically, but they have genuine warmth and love that are contagious. Some have achieved their big dreams—astronauts, doctors, or presidents of successful organizations—and seem to attract others. Some love God so much, they attract people—perhaps without those people even knowing why!

You can wear the most stylish clothes, apply makeup like a model, and wear impressive jewelry to try to attract other people. But unless you also have a positive, loving heart, you will never be really attractive to people. Attractiveness is a combination of things.

THE OUTER YOU
There is nothing wrong with looking "Great," "Fabulous," or "Stunning!" Do what you can to make your outer self look good. Study hairstyles, clothing styles, makeup, and so forth. Some people won't look beyond your physical appearance. Simply be aware there's more to being beautiful than just an attractive "package." Outer attractiveness alone isn't enough.

THE INNER YOU
You can try to improve the inner you in a couple of major ways. One is to deepen your relationship with God and closely model

your life according to the teaching of the Scriptures. Be honest. Be loving. Be obedient to God. Be an encourager and a biblical model to others.

The second way to develop the inner you is to find courses you can take. You can find many self-help books, tapes, and seminars available. Keep working on the inner you. It is a necessary element in the attractiveness formula.

YOUR DREAMS

Don't be afraid to dream big. If you decide you would like to be an astronaut, doctor, lawyer, or President of the United States, you can change your mind later if you wish. In college, people's majors change like the weather. However, I would encourage you to start by considering a career you'd enjoy doing—something that is interesting and attractive. And when people ask, "What are you going to do when you're on your own?" tell them, "I'm hoping to become an astronaut" (or whatever).

Imagine meeting someone for the first time. You ask, "Tom, what are you going to do after college?" He replies, "I don't have any idea. Maybe I'll just sort of work hourly, make enough to get by, and then bum around the country." But when you ask Joe the same thing, he says, "I'm planning to be a copyright lawyer and get involved in the music business." Which person would you find more attractive?

GOD'S BLESSING

"When a man's ways are pleasing to the Lord, he makes even his enemies live at peace with him" (Proverbs 16:7, NIV). When you live a godly life, even your enemies find you more attractive.

It makes good sense: If you work on your outside appearance, develop your inside appearance, follow your dreams, and live in a way that is pleasing to God, you will be an attractive person!

HOW WILL THIS APPLY WHEN I'M ON MY OWN?

Many adults have never understood this principle. They spend hundreds or thousands of dollars on European high-fashion clothes, exotic facial cleansers, and diamond jewelry. But such things rarely do anything to make them more attractive on the inside. It is only as you learn to balance these areas that you begin to become a more attractive, interesting person.

KEY QUESTIONS

1. *What three things can you do in the next 30 days to make your outer appearance more attractive? How about your inner character?*
2. *What might you choose as an attractive profession or hobby?*
3. *Are your ways pleasing to the Lord? If not, what can you change in the next 30 days?*

ACTION POINT

On a 3" x 5" card, make a list of things you'd like to change during the next 30 days. Carry the list in your pocket and read it every day for 30 days—maybe even several times a day. Keep focusing on how you would like to become a more attractive person.

PRINCIPLE 95

Discipline is saying yes to what you should do, and no to what you might want to do yet know you shouldn't.

Discipline is something we all struggle with because it is tied so closely to motivation. Most people who feel they have a discipline problem actually have a problem with motivation.

To illustrate: The alarm clock goes off and you're facing a long day of tests and homework assignments. It's hard to discipline yourself to get up, because it's all you can do to drag your bones out of bed! But if the day's plans include the amusement park or the start of summer vacation, you have no problem with the discipline it takes to get out of that same bed—even earlier in the morning! When you're highly motivated, discipline is never a problem. When you're not highly motivated, discipline is always a problem.

DISCIPLINE IS SAYING YES . . . AND NO

A person usually knows what he or she should do. We know when we should study, turn off the television set, refuse a third dessert, or whatever. Discipline is simply saying yes to what we should do.

Discipline always includes a teeter-totter decision between what we know we *ought* to do, and what we *want* to do, but know we shouldn't. The only way to say no to what we shouldn't do is by being highly motivated to say yes to what we know we *should* do.

We need ready answers. Without an adequate answer to the question, "Why should I get out of bed?" the price of getting up seems too high. Without an answer to, "Why should I say no to this piece of pie?" the price of discipline always appears unreasonable.

THE SOURCE OF MOTIVATION

If motivation is the key to developing discipline, where do we get motivation? It comes primarily from setting goals for the future. For example, why study if you're not going to use that information in the future to make the grades to get into a good college?

The clearer your goals for the future, the easier it is to keep yourself motivated. And once you establish motivation, the discipline to follow through on it becomes much easier.

Consider a runner training for the Olympics. He wakes up every morning with a goal clearly in mind—getting to the finish line first on the day he has his event. He is motivated to get out of bed early each morning. He is motivated to say no to pancakes and syrup for breakfast. He is motivated to run each morning whether he feels like it or not. And he has the strength to say yes to all the things he knows he must do to train properly.

The Olympic trainee has an adequate answer to the question "Why?" The price of "superhuman" discipline does not seem too high for him. Nor will it for you when you find the motivation—and the discipline—to do what you know you should do.

KEY QUESTIONS

1. *What goal do you have which makes you willing to give up something today for a better performance later?*
2. *Whenever you think about that goal, aren't you more highly motivated than normal? Do you find discipline much easier?*
3. *Where do you struggle most with discipline? What motivation can you find that would strengthen your discipline?*

ACTION POINT

Make a list of three major two-year goals you would be willing to give up most everything else for if necessary. (Getting into your favorite college? Buying a brand new sports car? Losing 15 pounds?) Think about your three goals and how important they are to you, then see if your motivation and discipline don't increase the next time something comes along that could get in the way of them.

"In everything, do to others what you would have them do to you" (Matthew 7:12, NIV).

Contained in this single Bible verse is the most reliable test of right and wrong for relationships. It is easy to tell if making fun of people or shutting them out of a social group is right or wrong. Simply ask yourself, "Would I want someone to do that to me?"

"Do unto others" isn't just a catchy saying. It is a command of God. Jesus instructs us to treat other people the way we want to be treated!

Recently I met with a friend I'll call Jerry, who had done a lot of design work for a particular client. The client was being extremely critical, informing Jerry that if he didn't do this, this, and this, the company wouldn't pay him *anything*! Jerry was so discouraged he was about to quit. His client was certainly not being fair. The client would not want to be treated that way if he were in the same position. And to make things worse, the client represented a Christian company! This "do unto others" command is not just for Sunday mornings. It applies to everyone and everything!

PUT YOURSELF IN THE OTHER PERSON'S PLACE
A good way to relate to other people is to ask yourself, "How would I want someone to relate to me?" If you don't know how to make friends with a new kid at school, consider, "How would I want someone to treat me if I were new?" Then treat the new student in exactly the way you would want to be treated. It's an easy way to know how to do just the right thing in a complex social relationship.

Put this principle high on your list of things to remember. Memorize it and live by it! "In everything, do to others what you would have them do to you."

KEY QUESTIONS
1. How do you like to be treated?
2. Have you been treating other people the way you like to be treated?
3. How can you put this principle to work right now?

ACTION POINT
Make a list of three things you would most like from other people (compliments, companionship, etc.). Then go give those things to *other* people. For example, if you like to be told you're attractive, tell someone she's pretty. If you feel lonely, don't wait for a friend— go become a friend! When you initiate the action, you'll experience the surprising results of the "do unto others" principle.

Whenever you feel insecure, think of others first!

Every person alive has gone through raging battles with insecurity (whether or not they show it). We all have struggled at one time or another with the problems of looking right, being accepted, or making embarrassing mistakes. The question is not, "Will I feel insecure?" The question is, "When and where will I feel insecure?"

WHEN INSECURITY STRIKES

You may be confident when playing athletics or music, yet feel very uncomfortable at a party. Others may be party animals, but insecure when performing a musical piece. Whenever you feel insecure (and it is absolutely guaranteed you will at some time), think of others first!

When you are at a party and are insecure about whether your outfit, makeup, or hairstyle will be acceptable, try this experiment: Stop thinking about yourself altogether. Rather, think of all the other people at the party and how insecure they must feel. Each person has certain physical characteristics (whether it's a big nose, big hips, unruly hair, big ears, small hands, big feet, etc.), which make him or her feel self-conscious. All of us have insecurities, and each person at the party feels as insecure as you do.

The Bible tells us, "Perfect love drives out fear" (I John 4:18, NIV). As you start thinking of others and imagining ways to make them feel confident, your own insecurity and anxiety will disappear.

Whenever you see a person with some obvious flaw in his image (a huge nose, for instance), comment on his hair, clothing, eyes, or some other positive quality. Try to put the person at ease. Look for ways to convey that the flaw is insignificant to you. As you accept people in spite of any imperfections, you will find that they give you the same freedom not to be perfect.

An old Russian proverb says, "When you meet a man, you judge him by his clothes. When you leave a man, you judge him by his heart." Quickly learn to see beyond a person's external image. Other people are just like you. They want to be accepted.

Adults have as many insecurities as teenagers! As a consultant, I deal with presidents of major companies and senior pastors from some of the largest churches. Many of these leaders still have overwhelming insecurities. Some say when they speak in front of a group of people, their voices tremble, their legs feel like rubber bands, and their throats get dry. They fear they won't represent the company well. If you can learn to put other people first, you may be able to avoid some of the problems these people face in their jobs.

A LESSON FOR THE TEACHER

One day I was driving to a conference with a client who is the president of a very significant Christian organization. He was 45 years old, but you would have thought he was 14 and going to his first party. He kept asking, "Do you think I look okay? Do you think my outfit is too showy? Do you think my shoes are all right? Do you think people will listen to what I have to say?" It was one of the most self-centered conversations I have ever heard in my entire life.

Finally I asked him, "How honest can I be with you right now?"

He replied, "As honest as you want to be."

I continued, "Do you want to know how much the people at this conference care about your clothes, your hair, your shoes, or how you look? Zero! They couldn't care less how you look. You could come in looking like a mess, but if you care about them, it won't matter. Everyone at the conference has serious troubles, doubts, and problems. If you focus on each individual's problems, you'll help them in ways you can't imagine. But if you go there with a self-conscious approach, you'll offend them. They will feel you don't care about them . . . only about yourself."

My honesty shocked him! But being a man eager to grow and learn, he immediately responded, "You're absolutely right. I have been self-centered, and I see what you're saying. I will try to do exactly what you have advised."

Two days after the conference he told me, "I can't believe what a needy group of people this was. All the people I talked to told me how they were struggling with something in their lives."

I asked him, "How many people seemed to care how your outfit looked?"

He said, "Surprisingly, not a single one. They just cared whether I was interested in them or not!"

Whenever you feel insecure, think of others first!

KEY QUESTIONS

1. *What are your greatest strengths? What do you do well? What do you really like about yourself?*
2. *What are the three things you would most like to change about yourself or make less obvious to people when you meet them?*
3. *How can you make other people feel more secure?*

ACTION POINT

Make a list of the strengths you have. Ask your parents and friends to add to the list. You may also want to ask each person, "What area of personal growth do I most need to work on?" (Don't ask them to list your bad points unless you are ready to hear what they have to say.)

"A gentle answer turns away wrath, but a harsh word stirs up anger"

(PROVERBS 15:1, NIV).

How many times have you seen someone respond with harsh statements, hand gestures, or demands when another person seems too slow or clumsy? When one person says something harsh and someone else flares back, the anger level just escalates.

I once heard a speaker suggest, "Be an absorber of pressure, not a reflector of it." He gave illustrations of how some people are able to absorb another person's anger rather than responding with more anger.

When people are angry with you or say harsh things, try to give them the benefit of the doubt. Learn not to take their insults personally. Assume they're just having a bad day. My brother-in-law, Jerry Bach, reminds himself, "Somewhere this person has a mother who loves him very much."

A GENTLE ANSWER

It's hard to say "I'm sorry" while you're being yelled at. But often these two little words will get a very positive response. The person may respond, "No, *I'm* sorry. I guess I was just blowing off steam."

Likewise, an angry response will definitely intensify the situation. It's safe to say that lashing back while angry has gotten more than one person fired. If you're being reprimanded by your boss, why not say, "I'm sorry. I didn't know how to do it right. I'll do it differently in the future." This lets the boss know you're willing to change. Don't become defensive and strike back with a smart remark.

Even when relatives or friends come at you with harsh words, diffuse the situation with a gentle answer if at all possible. When neither person is willing to respond with a gentle answer, a fight usually breaks out that may result in a broken relationship, or even a broken nose! What starts out as a simple difference of opinion can quickly become a shouting match when neither person is willing to back off.

HOW WILL THIS APPLY WHEN I'M ON MY OWN?
Sometimes harsh words break apart adult business relationships, corporations, partnerships, or marriages. Many times a husband or wife refuses to say, "I'm sorry. Let's work it out."

The older you get, the more critical it becomes to absorb other people's pressures and to respond with a gentle answer instead of angry words. Also, people who can't handle anger tend to become more vengeful with age. As teenagers, harsh words may lead to a fistfight. As adults, loud disagreements can erupt into murders, wars, divorces, major business errors and other severe problems.

While you're young, heed the wisdom of the wisest man who ever lived, King Solomon. He knew that, "A gentle answer turns away wrath, but a harsh word stirs up anger." It's still true today.

KEY QUESTIONS
1. *When have you seen this principle work in your life?*
2. *What experience have your parents had with this principle?*
3. *Have you recently given anyone a harsh answer?*

ACTION POINT
Make a list of people you have responded to harshly during the last few months. Go out of your way to ask forgiveness from those people. Tell them you are sorry you responded as you did, and that you'll try to be more gentle in future responses. You might be surprised how gentle their responses will be to you.

"Be prepared for the fact that life isn't fair . . . life is tough . . . life is full of hard knocks. When these times come, trust God and keep on keeping on!"

JERRY BACH

Probably one of the cruelest of all expectations is that life will be fair. As much as we'd like to think so, we just can't live with that illusion very long. Life has a way of sending us through the "school of hard knocks," and few of us are able to skip that class!

LIFE IS UNFAIR

If you think life is fair and everyone gets treated equally, you can expect a lot of frustration. The Declaration of Independence states that all men are created equal. But it never promises all people will be treated equally. As a matter of fact, that is an impossibility.

Even two children growing up in the same home are never truly treated equally. As much as a parent tries, it's not possible. Assume that you won't be treated equally to other people. In some cases you will be the advantaged person. In other situations someone else will be treated better than you. That's a part of life.

The quicker you see that life isn't fair, the easier it will be to deal with the times when you feel you've been treated unfairly.

LIFE IS TOUGH

It's interesting to note that young people who seem to have life easy often find it most difficult to adjust to the realities of adulthood. If you're having it somewhat tough as a teenager, be assured that you are maturing and growing in ways which will help you be stronger in adulthood.

Life is tough! Get used to it. See your tough times as growing times. And be sure to appreciate and be thankful for the times that seem easier.

LIFE IS FULL OF HARD KNOCKS
Sometimes when everything seems to be going right, disaster suddenly hits—a tornado, flood, fire, or car accident can destroy prized possessions or even take the life of someone you love. Life is simply full of hard knocks.

When hard times come, the key is not to blame God but to turn to Him. Scripture says that the rain falls on the just and the unjust (Matthew 5:45). Disasters occur due to laws of nature. If you are a victim, you should not interpret the event as punishment for some sin you've committed. It's just a period of "rain."

TRUST GOD
One day a man on the radio said, "When the world crumbles all around you and life seems to lie in shambles at your feet, there's not a lonelier man on the face of the earth than the man who has forgotten how to pray."

Talk to God every day. Then when hard times come, your trust and faith will be strong. Once you've prayed about a situation, do what wise grandparents and parents have said for centuries: "Keep on keeping on!" Learn to "put one foot in front of the other and just keep walking." Winston Churchill said it this way, "Sometimes our best is not enough; we must do what's required!"

HOW WILL THIS APPLY WHEN I'M ON MY OWN?
In going from living with my parents to living on my own, one thing I learned was that life doesn't get easier as you get older. It simply changes. Life still isn't fair. Life is still full of hard knocks. The only difference is, the knocks seem to come a little harder.

Learn early to turn to God and trust Him. Develop the discipline of "keeping on" during hard times. The lessons you learn and the Scriptures you memorize as a young person will all be of immense value when you experience the pressures of adulthood.

KEY QUESTIONS

1.*Have you been frustrated when life didn't seem fair?*
2.*In what ways does life seem unfair to you?*
3.*What can you do to overcome the "hard knocks" you've been given?*

ACTION POINT

Make a list of all the ways life has been more than fair to you. Consider your health, your clothes, your home, and your educational advantages over many people in the world. Keep this list handy for times when you need to be reminded of the positive advantages you've enjoyed. Review the list when it seems life has been just too tough.

PRINCIPLE

100

Each person on earth is as unique as a flake of snow. Recognize your uniqueness as a gift and find creative ways of making the most of it.

When people want to be accepted by "the group," they often try to be like everyone else. They conform in looks, speech, behavior, and dress! But true unity isn't achieved through conformity, but rather through diversity!

Imagine a football team with all quarterbacks, a baseball team with all pitchers, or a soccer team with all goalies. Trying to be like everyone else is just as impractical—and silly!

Look for the ways you are unique. Recognize the strength in those qualities. Don't see your uniqueness as a limitation or flaw.

ONE OF A KIND

You are like no other person in the world. You are an extremely complex organism. Think how boring it would be if everyone looked the same and had the same interests and abilities! Life would be so dreary—not to mention an absolute mess—if people didn't have an assortment of talents to get a variety of jobs done. It's good that everyone is different.

Your uniqueness is a gift from God. You have a specific genetic structure handed down from your one-of-a-kind parents. It makes you unique as a person. You have certain similarities (family characteristics and traits) passed on to you, but no one is exactly like you. Think of your uniqueness as a gift from your relatives as well as a gift from God. You are very special. You are exceptional in many ways!

CREATIVE UNIQUENESS

The word *unique* is sometimes used to describe things that are odd, bizarre, or strange. But an individual's uniqueness is better defined as wonderful, distinctive, and strong. It is something to be developed and appreciated. Make the most of it!

Remember the story of the ugly duckling? As a baby swan among baby ducks, its "uniqueness" made it stand out awkwardly—it had a too-long neck and too-big body among other problems. But as an adult, the swan was beautiful, graceful, and admired by everyone.

I'm sure many professional basketball players felt self-conscious at being so tall when they were in school. But they overcame those feelings and capitalized on their uniqueness. Discover how you are unique and find ways to make the most of what God has given you.

What is unique about you? Speaking ability? Speed? Size? A distinctive voice? People have made the most of these and other special talents to become successful in life. You can, too. Your uniqueness may not be a dominant strength, but you can still make it work for you. Keep asking yourself, "How can I maximize my uniqueness?"

Even if it hasn't happened yet, the day will come when people appreciate your true uniqueness. So don't think of yourself as an ugly duckling. You're a swan who simply hasn't been recognized yet.

KEY QUESTIONS

1. *How are you unique—different from other people?*
2. *How can you begin to make the most of that uniqueness?*
3. *Who else do you know who is unusually gifted in the same way you are?*

ACTION POINT

Define your greatest unique quality, even if you see it as a weakness rather than a strength. Ask at least ten people you trust (parents, grandparents, aunts, uncles, etc.) how they think you could turn that uniqueness into a strength.

APPENDIX

In this Appendix I have included additional materials and thoughts you may find helpful. It is my sincere hope that in moments of discouragement, you will be uplifted and strengthened by the words of someone who has been there. You're going to make it!

BRAINSTORMING QUESTIONS

These questions are good for thinking through any idea. They will help you develop more ideas by unlocking the unique creativity in your mind. They may prove especially valuable if you are serving on a committee at school, holding an office in student government, or trying to impress the boss at your first "real" job.

INSTRUCTIONS

(1) Before deciding on the practicality of any idea, get all of your ideas on the table by answering these 20 brainstorming questions.

(2) No matter how farfetched a new idea may be, write it down anyway. Nothing should be too silly to go on your list. If you're working with a group, you may want to have them respond to each suggestion with a rousing "Why not!"

(3) After you have lots of fresh new ideas on your list, then begin sorting out the "good ideas" from the "bad ideas" using the Idea Sorter questions that follow the Brainstorming questions.

(1)   What is the one word, one sentence, one paragraph essence of my idea (or program, project, department, etc.)?

(2)   Why am I doing what I'm doing?

(3)   What are my five most fundamental assumptions (in sequence)?

(4)   What changes would I make if I had unlimited time to accomplish the task? What if I had three years? Three days? Three hours? Three minutes?

(5)   Where will this idea be 10 years from now? 25 years? 100 years? 500 years?

(6)   What if I had unlimited help? Half my current staff? One or two extra people? What would the other people do? Why?

(7) What changes would I make if I had double my current budget? An unlimited budget? Half of my existing budget?

(8) How could I double the income or cut my costs in half?

(9) Which part of this idea warrants extra funding?

(10) Which part could I drop and not really miss?

(11) What is the ultimate "blue sky" potential of the idea?

(12) What five things could keep me from realizing the full potential? How can I clear away the roadblocks?

(13) What are my greatest strengths and how can I maximize them?

(14) If I had to start over, what would I do differently?

(15) What could happen if this idea is 100 times as successful as I have planned?

(16) What would it take to be number one in my entire field?

(17) Where will the market be in the year 2000?

(18) What 10 things do I want to accomplish in this area by the year 2000?

(19) How do I (or my team) feel the environment will have changed for this idea by the year 2000?

(20) In my most idealistic dreams, where will I (or my team) be in the year 2000?

IDEA SORTER LIST

These questions can help you sort your "good" ideas from your "great" ideas.

(1) Which idea best meets my needs (design parameters)?

(2) Which has the highest future potential?

(3) Which would be most cost effective in the long run?

(4) Which best fits my overall master plan?

(5) Which is most realistic for my staff today? Do we have the right project leader?

(6) Which could help us *win* rather than just *get by*?

(7) Which has the lowest up-front risk?

(8) Which would work best day to day?

(9) Which facts are still missing before I can properly decide?

(10) Which is really worth the overall risk involved?

(11) What are the predictable roadblocks?

(12) How does the senior executive and board (or anyone else I report to) feel about the project?

(13) Where would I get the funding to "Do it right"?

(14) Why have those who have tried similar ideas in the past failed?

(15) What are the side effects—good and bad—of the idea I am considering?

(16) Would I put my own money into this project or idea?

(17) Is the timing right?

(18) Can it be protected by trademark, patent, or copyright?

(19) Would I have to stop something I am now doing to take on this project?

(20) How can I test the idea before committing major resources to it?

DECISION-MAKING QUESTIONS

When you're on your own, you will often be faced with the need to make major decisions that could have life-changing consequences. It is of tremendous importance to learn how to make the best decisions possible by considering all the angles of a situation. Use these guidelines to help make the important decisions you are facing today. Adapt each question to your life situation as necessary.

(1) At its essence, in one sentence, what decision am I really facing? What is the bottom "bottom line"?

(2) Have I given myself 24 hours to let this decision settle in my mind?

(3) Am I thinking about this decision with a clear head, or am I fatigued to the point where I shouldn't be making major decisions?

(4) What would happen if I didn't do what I am planning to do?

(5) Is this the best timing? If not now, when?

(6) What difference will this decision make years from now?

(7) Am I dealing with a cause or a symptom? A means or an end?

(8) What would the ideal solution be in this situation?

(9) Who, what, when, where, why, how, how much?

(10) What are the key assumptions I'm making? (Cost, benefits, etc.)

(11) How will this decision affect my overall master plan? Will it get me off track?

(12) Is this different direction consistent with my historic values?

(13) Is this decision helping to maximize my key strengths?

(14) Should I seek outside counsel on this decision?

(15) How do I really feel about this decision?

(16) What are one to three alternative options?

(17) Should I write a policy about this type of decision in the future?

(18) What questions are lingering in my mind that are unresolved?

(19) Do I have peace of mind as I pray about this decision and look at it from God's eternal perspective?

(20) Can this decision be broken into smaller parts to be decided at a few "go" or "no go" points along the way?

(21) Is this what I would do if I had twice the budget? Half the budget? Five times as much time? One tenth the time? Twice as many staff people? Half the staff?

(22) What facts should I have before I can make this decision with total confidence?

(23) What would my top three most respected advisers suggest as I consider making this decision?

(24) How does my spouse and family feel about this decision?

(25) What does the Bible say about this decision?

(26) If I had to decide in the next two minutes, what would I decide? Why?

(27) Have I verified what the results have been for others as they have made this decision? Have I checked references? Have I interviewed previous users of the product or service?

(28) What trends, changes, or problems are making this change needed? How long do I expect these trends to last?

(29) Am I possibly hunting an elephant with a .22 caliber rifle, or a rabbit with an elephant gun?

(30) Are there any "hidden agendas" where someone is pushing for change for his or her own personal reasons?

A FINAL WORD

Leaving home to be on your own should be an exhilarating experience. Sure, there is probably a little fear involved, along with sadness
and other mixed emotions. But it should be a step into the challenge
of life—and you'll need all the help you can get.

Yet too many young people who leave home leave behind them
unresolved conflicts with one or both parents. The "on my own"
experience becomes more of an escape than a natural phase of life.
And sometimes the conflicts remain unresolved for years.

The conflicts may be primarily the young person's fault, or
perhaps it's mostly due to the parent(s), but more often than not
both parties are somewhat at fault. (I've talked with many parents
who express major disappointment in a child simply because they
didn't get what they expected. They wanted a frilly little girl and
got a tomboy instead. Or they expected a football star and got a
computer whiz kid who couldn't care less about sports.)

If you are leaving home to be on your own (or if you've already
gone), I strongly encourage you to resolve any conflicts that may
remain. I suggest you talk to God about your feelings, and then go

back and work things out with your parents and family. Sometimes you cannot talk with others to express how you really feel, but God is always there with a listening ear.

Perhaps your parents feel that they have not done a good job of raising you. This can be true of Christian parents as well as non-Christians. Awhile ago I saw a Christian psychologist on television. He was doing a national call-in survey of the attitudes of parents, both Christian and non-Christian. He was obviously expecting that Christian parents would see themselves as much more confident than non-Christian parents. To his surprise (and mine), the results were just the reverse of what he expected. Christian parents felt far more guilt and frustration than the non-Christian parents.

You see, few of the non-Christian parents had specific standards for their children to try to reach. On the other hand, most Christian parents had set such high standards for themselves (and their children) that there was no way anyone could possibly live up to their expectations. Therefore, they felt very inadequate as parents.

If you think about it, you and your parents will experience similar feelings when you leave home to be on your own. You will be somewhat uncertain of your new independence. Can you really succeed "out here" without the things you're accustomed to having done for you at home? At the same time, your parents are sure to feel a degree of worry for you and a sense of aloneness—even if you have brothers or sisters still at home. Your leaving will create an emptiness in both of you.

So what should you do? I think parents and their "on my own" children should become each other's biggest cheerleaders. They should forget the mistakes of their previous relationship and get busy affirming each other. You need to know that you have your parents' support as you go off to face the world. And they want to hear that you still love them and value their support and advice. That's why so many of the Action Points in this book included asking your parents for helpful information. Just because you are no longer in the same house with them is no reason to give up all that good (free) advice they can provide.

Sure, parents make mistakes. I know I did. In my early child-rearing days, I felt extraordinarily responsible for raising my children to be men and women of God and solid citizens. I kept trying to help them see how they could improve at every single point. I wanted to teach them how to do everything better. But they often interpreted my encouragement as criticism, and eventually began to feel they couldn't do anything right.

I appreciate that my children were honest with me about their feelings, and that they forgave me for being too ambitious. Since then I've tried to be a cheerleader five or ten times to every time I've been critical of something they've done.

I encourage you to be honest with your own parents, to work out any problems you may have between you, and to begin to encourage each other. You both need it, and it's a need that can't be filled by anyone else.

My final thought—remember the simple saying, which is timelessly profound:

You have one life twil' soon be past.
Only what's done for God will last.

PRINCIPLES CHECKLIST

❏ PRINCIPLE #1
Principles are mini-statements of cause and effect. Collect principles because they help explain why things do or do not work.

❏ PRINCIPLE #2
Everything in life fits into one of seven basic categories: Family/Marriage, Financial, Personal Growth, Physical, Professional/Career, Social, or Spiritual.

❏ PRINCIPLE #3
There is a huge difference between true love and "puppy love." Puppy love says, "You meet my needs." True love asks, "How can I meet your needs?"

❏ PRINCIPLE #4
It's essential to remember that more marriages end as a result of disagreement about money than any other reason.

❏ PRINCIPLE #5
In your early years of making money, live as frugally as possible in order that you may invest as much as possible.

❏ PRINCIPLE #6
Encouragement brings hope for the future. Specialize in encouraging.

❏ **PRINCIPLE #7**
People need encouragement and instruction more than criticism.

❏ **PRINCIPLE #8**
All miscommunications are the result of differing assumptions.

❏ **PRINCIPLE #9**
Love people and use things. Don't love things and use people.

❏ **PRINCIPLE #10**
Don't overlook old people. Here is wisdom and experience for our asking. Here, also, is a group to whom we must give kindness and affection.

❏ **PRINCIPLE #11**
When investing money, seek advice from those who have expertise in the area of your investment. Pay generously for that counsel. Scrutinize carefully advice from those who are selling.

❏ **PRINCIPLE #12**
Know what it costs you to live, and live within your means.

❏ **PRINCIPLE #13**
Borrow only for things that will increase in value. It is a losing battle to borrow for things that depreciate in value.

❏ **PRINCIPLE #14**
You can't win 'em all. You will have financial discouragements, setbacks, and disappointments, but . . . this phrase will help you over the rough places of your life.

❏ **PRINCIPLE #15**
Don't spend money you don't have.

❏ **PRINCIPLE #16**
When investing for future equity appreciation, always look for location and path of progress!

❏ PRINCIPLE #17

People who make money extremely fast usually lose it or spend it all. People who make money over a longer period of time tend to keep it.

❏ PRINCIPLE #18

It is extremely difficult to make your fortune in a salaried position. . . . If you want to make a real fortune, you have to come up with a product, idea, or service that is in demand or required by the masses.

❏ PRINCIPLE #19

Never turn down anything that's free.

❏ PRINCIPLE #20

Making money requires motivation. . . . Determine early what you want to use money for, and make that your goal. Never make your goal just money.

❏ PRINCIPLE #21

Investigate and gather as much information about an investment as possible. Remember nothing is free (financially) despite what anyone tells you.

❏ PRINCIPLE #22

How much in? How much out? When? More return is better than less. Sooner is better than later. Simple is better than complex. "For sure" is better than "Maybe."

❏ PRINCIPLE #23

Money is a means, not an end.

❏ PRINCIPLE #24

When you are thinking of making any investment, take 24 hours to "sleep on it." Think about the investment nonemotionally.

❏ PRINCIPLE #25

In purchasing anything (generally over $100), hear at least three salespeople tell their stories. *Copyright © 1991 by Bobb Biehl*

❑ PRINCIPLE #26
Risk only what you can afford to lose.

❑ PRINCIPLE #27
Start saving money now. People think in order to save a lot of money, you have to make a lot of money. In reality, acquiring a substantial sum of money requires only two things; time, and the discipline to consistently work toward a goal.

❑ PRINCIPLE #28
I have known many who could make money, but not many who could hang onto it. The people who can retain wealth once earned, and increase it, are the ones to observe.

❑ PRINCIPLE #29
One of the realities of life is that if you can't trust a person at all points, you can't truly trust him or her at any point.

❑ PRINCIPLE #30
We must deal with the circumstances as they are, not as we wish they were. Failure is assured when we practice denial, when we refuse to face reality. Be absolutely ruthless with yourself with regard to recognizing, facing up to, and dealing with hard realitites.

❑ PRINCIPLE #31
Your teachability will remain one of the bedrock issues for you to make the most of . . . making money and then in the management of that money after you have it.

❑ PRINCIPLE #32
Hard work is critical. . . . Successful people . . . work harder than the others. It is not luck. It is not coincidence. It is not inheritance. It is not contacts. It is hard work!

❑ PRINCIPLE #33
When you're bored, it's time to use your creativity rather than blaming someone else for your condition.

❏ PRINCIPLE #34
You can't win 'em all. You can't have it all. You don't want it all.

❏ PRINCIPLE #35
Don't be a "me, too" person. Learn to think and speak for yourself.

❏ PRINCIPLE #36
Good manners should be part of both masculine and feminine development.

❏ PRINCIPLE #37
Master the art of being positive. No one enjoys being with negative complainers!

❏ PRINCIPLE #38
A mistake is only a failure . . . if you don't learn from it.

❏ PRINCIPLE #39
Life without goals is like a race without a finish line.

❏ PRINCIPLE #40
Listen to God. Listen to yourself. Listen to trusted family and friends. And ignore the crowd.

❏ PRINCIPLE #41
To feel organized, have a place for everything, and everything in its place.

❏ PRINCIPLE #42
Success is the feeling you get when you reach your goals!

❏ PRINCIPLE #43
No body is perfect . . . accept yours!

❏ PRINCIPLE #44
Form healthy habits while you are young!

❏ PRINCIPLE #45
Take a shower a day . . . or friends (and dates) stay away!

❏ PRINCIPLE #46
Find a sport that fits you!

❏ PRINCIPLE #47
Sports are a vital element of our lives, but should never become the main goal of life.

❏ PRINCIPLE #48
Flee from sexual immorality.

❏ PRINCIPLE #49
When you see a person with a handicap, focus on the person more than the handicap!

❏ PRINCIPLE #50
Fatigue makes cowards of us all.

❏ PRINCIPLE #51
"Who of you by worrying can add a single hour to his life? Since you cannot do this very little thing, why do you worry about the rest?" (Luke 12:25, 26)

❏ PRINCIPLE #52
Learn to look people in the eyes both when you listen to and when you talk to them.

❏ PRINCIPLE #53
Nothing is meaningful without a context or comparison.

❏ PRINCIPLE #54
Once the facts are clear, the decisions jump out at you.

❏ PRINCIPLE #55
Efficiency is doing things right. Effectiveness is doing right things.

❑ PRINCIPLE #56

Leadership is knowing what to do next, knowing why that's important, and knowing how to bring the appropriate resources to bear on the need at hand.

❑ PRINCIPLE #57

When things seem overwhelming, make a list of all the things you've got to do, put them in order of importance, and start at the top.

❑ PRINCIPLE #58

Deciding what *not* to do is just as important as deciding what to do.

❑ PRINCIPLE #59

Everyone must take risks, but planning and research helps reduce the number of unnecessary and unwise risks you take.

❑ PRINCIPLE #60

Ultimately you can break every system into four steps: Input, Process, Output, and Feedback.

❑ PRINCIPLE #61

Invest your time wisely. Spend 80 percent of the time where you are the strongest, 15 percent on learning new things, and 5 percent in areas where you need or want to grow.

❑ PRINCIPLE #62

A picture is worth a thousand words . . . and a graph or chart is worth ten thousand numbers.

❑ PRINCIPLE #63

An activity is only work when you'd rather be doing something else.

❑ PRINCIPLE #64

Whatever profession you go into, it's good to pick something that looks real interesting. Get the right education, and go for it!

❏ PRINCIPLE #65
Select a job you like irregardless of the initial pay. . . . Those who enjoy their work approach it with enthusiasm and integrity, usually rising to the top of their profession, and receive good compensation for their services.

❏ PRINCIPLE #66
Most of your business opportunities or career positions will be obtained through personal contacts. Now is the time for you to develop a personal network.

❏ PRINCIPLE #67
For special gifts or services, make a game of saying "thank you" at least three different ways.

❏ PRINCIPLE #68
If you want to lose friends quickly, start bragging about yourself; if you want to make and keep friends, start bragging about others.

❏ PRINCIPLE #69
Concentrate on caring, not just conversations.

❏ PRINCIPLE #70
Never promise to keep a secret that will hurt someone.

❏ PRINCIPLE #71
The best way to make a good friend is to be a good friend.

❏ PRINCIPLE #72
You can feel lonely in a crowd. You can also be all alone and not feel lonely.

❏ PRINCIPLE #73
Make a lifelong game of remembering names! People appreciate it.

❏ PRINCIPLE #74
What you believe about people in general influences your behavior

and attitudes toward individuals. You should assume that people: (1) do what makes sense to them; (2) don't want to fail; (3) want to make a difference; (4) want to grow; and (5) need to be encouraged.

❏ PRINCIPLE #75
When you are proud and stuck-up, everyone is happy when you fail. When you are humble and serving, everyone is happy when you succeed.

❏ PRINCIPLE #76
If you know how to ask good questions and listen, you will never run out of great conversations.

❏ PRINCIPLE #77
Make asking and collecting questions a lifelong hobby.

❏ PRINCIPLE #78
By yourself you are alone, but with a friend you're a team of two.

❏ PRINCIPLE #79
If you can't trust everything a person says, you can't trust anything he or she says.

❏ PRINCIPLE #80
When visiting away from home, eat what you're fed, sleep where you're put, and always say "thank you!"

❏ PRINCIPLE #81
We all learn most from friends, not enemies. If you want to convince a person of something, first become a real friend . . . then present your case.

❏ PRINCIPLE #82
When you influence a child, you influence a life. When you influence a father, you influence a family. When you influence a pastor, you influence a church. When you influence a leader, you influence all who look to him or her for leadership.

❏ PRINCIPLE #83

Needs which make you weep or pound the table wake up and unlock your creativity.

❏ PRINCIPLE #84

In a business decision, the wise man considers the effect on all of the people involved, not just the profit for himself.

❏ PRINCIPLE #85

The poor can act as our guides through the eye of the needle. When we help them, we find self-fulfillment and the wisdom that leads to the joys of the kingdom of God.

❏ PRINCIPLE #86

Before you trust a man or his message, study his life.

❏ PRINCIPLE #87

God's Word, the Bible, is the world's only completely trustworthy measuring stick for truth. Without the Bible, there is no absolute standard of right or wrong.

❏ PRINCIPLE #88

When God seems far away, focus on biblical answers that cannot be questioned rather than life's questions that cannot be answered.

❏ PRINCIPLE #89

He is no fool who gives that which he cannot keep, to gain that which he cannot lose.

❏ PRINCIPLE #90

Ultimately we do everything for one of two reasons: To serve ourselves, or to serve God.

❏ PRINCIPLE #91

God's timing is perfect.

❑ PRINCIPLE #92

Giving to God and others is like the farmer planting seed. The more he plants, the greater his harvest.

❑ PRINCIPLE #93

Assume God and people like you, and things will work out.

❑ PRINCIPLE #94

Your attractiveness is a combination of the outer you, the inner you, your dreams, and God's blessing.

❑ PRINCIPLE #95

Discipline is saying yes to what you should do, and no to what you might want to do yet know you shouldn't.

❑ PRINCIPLE #96

"In everything, do to others what you would have them do to you" (Matthew 7:12).

❑ PRINCIPLE #97

Whenever you feel insecure, think of others first!

❑ PRINCIPLE #98

"A gentle answer turns away wrath, but a harsh word stirs up anger" (Proverbs 15:1).

❑ PRINCIPLE #99

Be prepared for the fact that life isn't fair . . . life is tough . . . life is full of hard knocks. When these times come, trust God and keep on keeping on!

❑ PRINCIPLE #100

Each person on earth is as unique as a flake of snow. Recognize your uniqueness as a gift and find creative ways of making the most of it.

Bobb Biehl is the president of Masterplanning Group International. To receive a copy of Masterplanning Group's complete resource catalog or to order any of the resources listed below, write to:

Bobb Biehl
Masterplanning Group/Resources
Box 952499
Lake Mary, Florida 32795

Or call:
Resource Order Desk: 1-800-443-1976
FAX: 1-407-330-4134

The following field tested resources from Masterplanning Group are listed alphabetically for easy reference.

ASKING TO WIN!

This booklet (part of our Pocket Confidence series) goes in your suit coat pocket, briefcase or purse. It contains 100 profound questions. Ten questions to ask in each of the following situations:

    1.   ASKING . . . profound personal questions and avoiding small talk.
    2.   BRAINSTORMING . . . your way out of a mental rut and maximizing your finest ideas!
    3.   CAREER-ING . . . when you, or a friend, are considering a career change.
    4.   DECIDING . . . when a risky, pressurized, costly decision needs to be made.
    5.   INTERVIEWING . . . getting behind a person's smile, and beyond her/his resume!
    6.   FOCUSING . . . or re-focusing your life.
    7.   ORGANIZING . . . your life to maximize your time!
    8.   PARENTING . . . to raise healthy, balanced children.
    9.   PLANNING . . . Masterplanning any organization or major project.
    10. SOLVING . . . any problem faster, with a systematic problem solving process.

Whenever you have a tough situation . . . ask profound questions to get profound answers and make wise decisions.

CAREER CHANGE QUESTIONS/LIFEWORK
30 questions to Ask Before Making Any Major Career Change

This series of thirty questions comes in handy any time you are thinking about the possibility of making a career change. Also, a practical counseling aid for friends in career transition. You hand them these questions; they may take hours to answer the questions, but will come to well thought-out answers. These questions save you hours of uncertainty. Is your current position JUST A JOB, your next CAREER MOVE, or your LIFE WORK? If you are uncertain, these profoundly simple ideas can help. This is priority reading for any reevaluating person ages twenty-five to sixty. A proven resource!

EVENT PLANNING (SUCCESSFUL) CHECKLIST
by Ed Trenner

This comprehensive 300-point checklist can cut your planning time in half, especially if you are new to planning special events. This checklist is designed for those who receive great pleasure from precision and for those who have yet to experience it. The 300-point checklist helps you keep from overlooking an obvious question and finding "egg on your face" at the event. This is a practical, proven, easy-to-use resource!

FOCUSING YOUR LIFE

Life often gets foggy, confused, and overwhelming. *Focusing Your Life* simplifies life! *Focusing Your Life* is a simple, step-by-step process you learn in about three hours, which helps clear the fog and keeps you focused for the rest of your life. This great personal retreat guide helps you reflect on your future! *Focusing Your Life* has been used by over 4,000 people to help form a crystal-clear direction in life. Let this resource help you FOCUS and SIMPLIFY your life.

HEART TO HEART MARRIAGE SERIES
Bobb and Cheryl Biehl

Whether you're about to pop the question, or popped it years ago, answering the questions in the Heart To Heart marriage series will be a great way to communicate with your mate. Asking each other these fresh questions will also identify possible trouble spots in your relationship and show you how to deal with them before they threaten your marriage.

Each of the books contains approximately 250 questions stimulating many heart-to-heart conversations, covering the seven basic areas of life. And each book has detailed steps for resolving disagreements.

Wonderful gifts for any friend whose marriage could benefit from a little more heart-to-heart communication.

Pre-marriage Questions,
GETTING TO REALLY KNOW YOUR LIFE MATE-TO-BE

These are the heart-to-heart questions you ask before you say "I Do", to make sure this is the right person for you. I hope you have found just the right person. But, just in case, it is far better to break an engagement than a marriage. Most couples find that they have far more in common than they had even realized. The handful of major disagreements can be discussed before the marriage to see if they are major differences which are "engagement breakers" or if they are just uncomfortable differences.

If you know someone who is about to be married and you feel that the marriage could be a disaster . . . but you can't say so or it would make the person want to get married even more. . . this is a great gift from your church to the couple.

Newly Married Questions,
MAKING THE MOST OF YOUR HONEYMOON YEAR

If any of your friends are in their first few years of marriage, especially their first year, and you sense that they may be having a few fundamental differences, this book can really help identify these points before they grow into marriage-threatening issues. It is far easier for them to address these questions while they are still in the honeymoon period of marriage. These questions spark wonderful fireside chats.

Anniversary Questions
KEEPING YOUR MARRIAGE HEALTHY AND SIZZLING

Give these questions to any couple who want to maximize a great marriage. Freshens, rekindles, maximizes heart-to-heart communication. These questions can also add very specific definition to any differences which are under the surface, before they become major problems. Great for long weekends together, long road trips, or vacation conversation. Also makes interesting meal conversation for older couples who have run out of things to talk about now that their children are gone. A very appropriate and beneficial church gift for any anniversary—first to seventy-fifth!

Pre-Marriage Questions
HELPING YOU START AGAIN

Any couple who are about to remarry have certain delicate questions they would desperately like to ask each other, but would find asking "out of the blue" very uncomfortable. By systematically going through all of the questions in this book even the most delicate questions can be approached with "the next question is . . .". As you know, most couples in the process of marrying again because of death or divorce want to avoid making mistakes in this new marriage. Whether their first marriage was the best marriage of the century, or was one of the worst disasters of the decade, these heart-to-heart questions help them enter their next marriage with eyes wide open!

LEADERSHIP CONFIDENCE

Approximately 3,800 people have completed the Leadership Confidence series. A wise, proven investment in your own future. This series is a life-long reference covering thirty essential leadership areas, including:

HOW TO COPE WITH: Change, Depression, Failure, Fatigue, Pressure.

HOW TO BECOME MORE: Attractive, Balanced, Confident,

Creative, Disciplined, Motivated.

HOW TO DEVELOP SKILLS IN: Asking, Dreaming, Goal Setting, Prioritizing, Risk Taking, Influencing, Money Managing, Personal Organization, Problem Solving, Decision Making, Communicating.

HOW TO BECOME MORE EFFECTIVE IN: Delegating, Firing, Reporting, Team Building, People Building, Recruiting, Masterplanning, Motivating.

A great track for you to use as a leadership development program.

MENTORING (Book)
Confidence in Finding A Mentor and Becoming One

If you would like to be a mentor, or find a mentor, but don't know where to start, this is it! This book explains clearly and completely what mentors do and don't do, the nature of the mentor-protégé relationship, the most common roadblocks to effective mentoring, and much more.

Mentoring is an invaluable way of teaching skills, traditions, and cultural nuances that can't be captured in the classroom. It helps you (as protégé) reach your full potential, and gives you (as mentor) the satisfaction of seeing your experience and ideals carried forward to the next generation. Mentoring is something anyone can do—but not everyone should do. This book shows you that being a successful mentor doesn't require perfection, and finding a mentor is probably much easier than you think. Mentoring can make a major difference in your life.

MENTORING (Booklet)
How to Find a Mentor and How to Become One
Bobb Biehl and Glen Urquhart

Without a mentor a person often feels under-powered, as if not living up to her or his true potential. A mentoring relationship can easily add 30-50% extra "life and leadership horsepower" to any person. This booklet gives you many useful how-to steps for forming a mentoring relationship, and answers practical mentoring questions with life-proven answers.

NOTE: To request a free <u>Mentoring Today</u> newsletter, call the resource order desk at the number given above.

MENTORING WISDOM

Approximately 200 *quotable* leadership principles, rules of thumb, and observations which are key to generating creative ideas and gaining objective perspective! Add your own principles over the next twenty to thirty years. Build it for a lifetime, then pass it on to help all who look to you for leadership—children, grandchildren, and protégés.

ROLE PREFERENCE INVENTORY

The Role Preference Inventory (sixth edition—seventeenth printing since 1980) is a proven way of understanding yourself better. In simple language it lets you tell your spouse, your friends, or your colleagues what makes you tick, what turns you on, what burns you out! The Role Preference Inventory clarifies what you really want to do—not what you have to do, have done the most, or think others expect you to do. It is the key to understanding personal fulfillment and is an affordable way of building strong team unity by predicting team chemistry. This profoundly simple, self-scoring, self-interpreting inventory is the key to selecting the right person for the right position, thus helping avoid costly hiring mistakes.

STOP SETTING GOALS
By Bobb Biehl

Do you hate setting goals, or know someone who does? Then this book is for you!

"I no longer feel like a second class citizen!" is the most common reaction to this idea. This simple idea has already freed thousands of people. As a team leader you can reduce team tensions by 50%

while simultaneously increasing team spirit by 50%, by introducing this simple idea at your next staff meeting. Any leader who understands and implements this idea will make her/his team leader, board, or stockholders very happy with the results!

STRATEGY WORK SHEETS (11" x 17")

This quick, systematic, step-by-step tool helps you think through a solid success strategy for each of your goals. Use these sheets for turning each major goal into a realistic plan. Strategy Work Sheets help you spot problems in basic thinking and strategy before those problems become costly.

THE QUESTION BOOK
By Bobb Biehl

DECISIONS, DECISIONS, DECISIONS!

Don't make a major or stressful decision again without asking yourself these profound questions! Ninety-nine experts give you the twenty questions they would teach their own sons or daughters to ask before making an important decision in their area of expertise.

The Question Book is a life-long reference book for you. Written in a style to last a lifetime, it will never really be outdated. These questions reduce the stress of making a risky decision in a field in which you have little or no experience. This wise investment saves many dollars over the years. You can save thousands, if not millions, of dollars by knowing how to make wise decisions while under stress, pressure, or emotional manipulation.

WHY YOU DO WHAT YOU DO
By Bobb Biehl

This book is a result of over 21,000 hours of behind-the-defenses experiences with some of the finest, (emotionally healthy) Christian leaders of our generation. This model was developed to maximize the potential of "healthy" people who have a few emotional mysteries still unanswered!

Why do I have a phobic fear of failure, rejection or insignificance?

Why am I so driven to be admired, recognized, appreciated, secure, respected, or accepted?

Why am I an enabler, leader, promoter, rescuer, controller, people pleaser?

Why am I a perfectionist, workaholic, or "withdrawer" from tough situations?

Why are pastors vulnerable to affairs? Where am I the most vulnerable to temptation? How do I guard against temptation?

Why do I have such a hard time relating to my parents when I love them so much?

Why do they sometimes seem like such children?

This book helps basically healthy people understand these and other emotional mysteries in the silence of their own hearts, without years of therapy.

WISDOM FOR MEN
By Bobb Biehl

Life principles combined with parallel scriptures to give wise perspective on many topics. Easy to read format. Great relaxation reading—relax and stretch at the same time. Gift book (birthday, Christmas, Father's Day, graduation, etc.) for any man!

WRITING YOUR FIRST BOOK!

If you have been wanting to start writing a book but still haven't actually started a manuscript, let *Writing Your First Book!* be your starting point. This is a skeleton outline—no complicated, sophisticated theory or double-talk. It is just a bare bones, easy-to-follow, step-by-step checklist to becoming a royalty-receiving author. A wise investment in your own future.